A Holistic Guide to the Power of Your Voice

"This is a skill everybody should have, just like brushing your teeth."
Best-selling author Jack Canfield

Sing Yourself Well™
in 7 Seconds

The 7 Second Reset™
How to FREE Your VOICE -
and Change Your LIFE!

Ulrike Selleck

© Copyright 2025 by Ulrike Selleck. All rights reserved. Printed in the United States of America. Except as permitted under the United States Copyright Act of 1976, no part of this publication may be reproduced or distributed in any form or by any means, or stored in a database or retrieval system, without the prior written permission of the publisher.

Disclaimer: The information contained in this publication is intended to be educational, and should in no way be construed to mean replacing any common sense measures, nor medical or psychological advice, diagnosis, or treatment. The author and publisher make no claim as to the completeness or accuracy of the information contained within. The author is not responsible for the wellbeing of anyone who buys this book or follows its instructions.

ISBN 978-0-9978491-0-3

Wellness, Voice, Health, Healing, Singing, Yoga, Empowerment, Meditation, Education

Cover illustrations by Shoo Rayner

Congratulations!

You're holding in your hands the book that'll allow you to take charge of Your Health, Happiness & Vitality by Expressing Your Voice today!

In this Book You'll Discover

- The quick, proven 7 Second Reset to get your energy moving, feel joy, and increase your vitality.
- The Why, What, & How to using Your Voice the way Nature intended, for your full self-expression and freedom.
- The 7 Qualities you need for your health, strength & wellbeing—and how to make them manifest in your body starting today!

For the online **Sing Yourself Well**™ Video Training of The 7 Second Reset™, all 7 Steps, plus 7 Bonuses, go to SingYourselfWell.com.

You can watch, listen and follow along. Plus if you want to refer back or fast forward, you may do so at your leisure.

See you there and Sing Yourself Well! :)
~ Ulrike Selleck, Voice Expert

Table of Contents

Acknowledgment vii

About the Author ix

The Healing Power of the Human Voice xi

Part 1: The Reasons You Need to Get Motivated 1

Chapter 1: Introduction - Why and How You Can Reverse
Cause and Effect 3

Chapter 2: How to Get the Most out of This Book 9

Chapter 3: Who Should Read This? This is for You, If... 13

Chapter 4: When and How It All Happened: My Sing
Yourself Well Story 25

Chapter 5: Why We Don't Sing 37

Chapter 6: Why We Need to Sing - Your Voice Shapes
Your and Our World 45

Chapter 7: Why We Breathe 53

Chapter 8: The Seven Qualities of True Wellness You Must
Have to Improve Your Life, Love, Health,
and Happiness 57

Part 2: The How To 63

Chapter 9: 1 Awareness 65

Chapter 10: 2 Relaxation 69

Chapter 11: 3 Alignment 77

Chapter 12: 4 Expansion 89

Chapter 13: 5 Flow 97

Chapter 14: 6 Power And Empowerment 103

Chapter 15: 7 Energy 113

Part 3: Your Healing Bonuses 125

Bonus #1: Self Love 127

Bonus #2: Intuition 101 135

Bonus #3: Feel It & Heal It 147

Again: Conclusion and Send Off! 161

Acknowledgments 167

Acknowledgment

Thank you, Divine, for guiding me in writing this book. Dear Reader, you'll find specific acknowledgments at the end of this book.

About the Author

#1 Best-selling author and TEDx speaker Ulrike Selleck, is a seasoned voice expert with 25 years experience, a classical singer, voice teacher, mentor, speaker, mother, artist, and intuitive healer. She holds a B.A. in Psychology from MIU, is an energy healer, as well as a Transcendental Meditation (TM) teacher. Her TEDx talk was on September 12 2025, at Wilson Park, AL.

When experiencing a traumatic health crisis at age 32, Dr. Deepak Chopra told Ulrike to free her voice, learn to sing, and speak up. Since then she has been singing, learning, teaching, healing, and performing for thousands, and is passionate about showing people from all over the world how to use the power of their voice.

Ulrike's loving, spontaneous, and exuberant nature integrates a fun, practical, spiritual approach with an earthy, easy to understand teaching style. Even though a quintessential introvert, Ulrike loves performing, arranging, and recording classical arias with percussion, Jazz and Rap, as in her original arrangement and rendition of Handel's "Rejoice!" She lives in the Iowa countryside with her man, her paints, and 9 cats.

The Healing Power of the Human Voice

"This Sing Yourself Well™ 7 Second Reset™ is so simple and so profound. Parents can use it to help their children. I promise you, this is a skill everybody should have, just like brushing your teeth." Jack Canfield, Best-Selling Author

How many of us have been told, "You can't sing, you have a terrible voice"? Or, "Shut up, be quiet, not so loud, sshhh"? Yes. So many of us!

Research (conducted at the University of California, Harvard Medical School, and Northwestern University) shows that when we get negative feedback on our voice, or are told to be quiet—especially as kids and adolescents—it can lower our self-esteem, increase anxiety, and even impact our mental and physical health!

Today, I want to share an idea with you that may just change your life. No matter what you've been told, or whether you think you can sing, you can, even now, use your voice to feel happy, energized, and confident in just seconds. There's a reset process so powerful that when best-selling author Jack Canfield tried it, he told me, "This is a skill everybody should have, just like brushing your teeth."

You might not be aware that you are, even now, sitting on a gold mine: your own, unique voice. When we say the eyes are the window to the soul, I would also say that it is the voice that offers the best view into the human condition.

Stay with me, for a moment.

Feeling the energy in your dentist's office, eavesdropping on the conversations in the waiting room, you can observe people making small talk, using a somewhat strained, trying-to-be-friendly, quiet, tense, and even fearful voice.

Listening to a jealous lover—or being one yourself—you might find his or her voice suddenly erupting, almost out-of-control loud, and full of emotion.

Hearing children play in the yard, their high pitched laughter and varied tones of voice charm your heart. Until, of course, they eventually annoy the heck out of you, coming across as too shrill, too loud, and altogether too much for where you're at.

According to studies people experiencing depression, for example, have a fundamentally different voice from people who are happy and content. Their voice is more monotonous, mirroring the state of seeming hopelessness they feel inside. In fact, I've observed that when we speak and aren't feeling well, we often only use about 20%, 7-8 notes of our vocal range!

But our body is an instrument that has on average 40 notes! Meaning, we don't use about 80% of our voice, of the frequencies available to each of us. No wonder we're often depressed, anxious, or unwell.

From even just these examples you can see that the condition and tone of our voice are altered by how we feel.

Our voice communicates who we are and how we feel at any given moment. And our breath embodies who we allow ourselves to be.

So what *is* it about the voice that allows us to express such a huge range of emotions?

It turns out each tone has a different frequency, and requires different amounts and qualities of breath. For example, if you feel sad, your voice will reflect that state according to the quality and density of your breath, and the frequency and quality of your tone.

But here comes the magic: you aren't helpless!

You can take control of your life through your breath, your voice and, along with it, your emotions! How? By starting from the other end!

If your voice expresses your emotions, taking control of your voice can alter your emotions. All in a natural, effortless way—long forgotten, and sadly never taught in schools today.

You can actually breathe the full potential of your breath, allow yourself to be the person you want to be, and express the tones of this new person you are becoming—all with your voice.

The result? You'll feel different—freer, more empowered, healthier and happier. When you naturally culture your real, unique, full voice, you're able to choose from a *veritable smorgasbord* of tools and emotions already at your disposal, even now.

This is what this book is all about. Sing Yourself Well provides you with the fundamental knowledge and basic skills to use your voice fully. You see, when we want to change something about ourselves, it has to be manifested from within, with the abilities we already possess.

Simply saying affirmations until we're blue in the face will not accomplish nearly as much. Instead, the energetic frequencies available to you already have to be transformed into matter.

ULRIKE SELLECK

This book shows you exactly how—in just a **few seconds at a time**—you can turn your body, breath, and voice into the ultimate healing tool. You can allow yourself to be who and how you really want to be: fearless, whole, healthy, joyful, happy, full of energy, powerful, and free. Most of all: the best possible version of your unique self.

Then, when you put affirmations on top of **that**—now that is powerful!

PART 1

THE REASONS YOU NEED TO GET MOTIVATED

CHAPTER 1

Introduction - Why and How You Can Reverse Cause and Effect

The 21st century has presented us with more conveniences than ever before, and yet so many of us are still less than happy with our lives.

Maybe you already practice meditation, do yoga, exercise regularly, eat healthy, and get enough sleep (well, more or less), but there's still this heaviness that bogs you down from time to time.

Well, let me ask you a question:

Do you sing? And by sing, I mean regularly, with your whole body and full lung capacity? Really going all-out, like an opera singer?

No?

It's okay. The majority of people—for a variety of reasons I'll share with you in a little while—don't sing nearly as often as they would like. But now, no matter your past justifications for not using your full voice:

- It's time for you to speak up. To speak out. To sing out!
- It's time for you to reclaim the full range and ability of your voice.
- It's time for you to express who you are.

No matter what people have told you in the past, you're entitled to use your full body, your full instrument, the full 100% of your voice.

So, you may say: "I can't sing on key. I never learned. Singing is not my thing. I don't have time."

But you don't need to spend years training your voice to experience the positive benefits it can give you—I've already done that part for you. You just need to know **how** to use your voice fully in your daily life.

There are **seven key qualities** your voice is able to express, and once you have all of them down pat, you're good to go! Your health, energy, happiness, strength, and yes, even your relationships, all will improve.

"The reason I contacted Ulrike was really that my relationship was in trouble. We had both hired lawyers, and we were on our way to divorce. I felt I wanted to make one more effort to see if we could avoid that. To my surprise, along with her personal guidance, Ulrike had both of us learn the Sing Yourself Well™ 7 Second Reset™. It was astonishing. We both, individually, and together as a couple felt freer, stronger, and more loving every time we did it. And it only took a few seconds each time. Well, what do I tell you: we're still married." S.L., Mother, I.C., IA.

More good news? Once you've really learned this, you'll be able to unleash the full potential of your voice in just **seven seconds** any time you need or want to, for the rest of your life!

"I have a smile on my face and feel really grounded. These tools get me feeling so good. They are fabulous for singing, acting, communication, and total life style." S.M., Yoga Instructor, N.Y. City, NY.

Often, when we use only a small part our voice's potential, we're simply not able to live our full potential. That can express itself as lethargy, a weak immune system, insecurity, or a feeling of being trapped, and all of that translates in less than fulfilling relationships.

"I had felt so sad that my daughter had not been in contact with me in years, despite my reaching out to her repeatedly. Ulrike was very clear that in my session we would only work on me, not my daughter. I felt such relief even just from doing the simple exercises she had me do (plus her intuition was right on!). But imagine my surprise and delight, when, out of the blue, I got a call from my daughter the next day—barely 18 hours after my session with Ulrike! The only thing I had done differently was my healing session with Ulrike, and practicing the simple 7 Second Reset™ she taught me. Curiously, ever since then, my business is doing better, too! I am beyond grateful, and I still do the exercises to this day." T.N., Entrepreneur and Company Owner, S.F., CA.

After all, the first relationship is with ourselves. If that is good and clear, that energy will radiate and influence all other relationships.

If that is compromised, it influences all other interactions as well:

- Research has shown that the voice of people with depression changes. It has less vitality, less variety, less melody, and more monotony.
- When we're feeling depressed or insecure, we have less choice.
- Insecurity is reflected in our voice; it sounds weak.
- Our health suffers, and our lung capacity is less.
- Our immune system becomes weaker, and our overall strength lessens.
- Our life expectancy decreases.

Now that we know our voice is susceptible to change from emotional and physical agents…

What if we tackled the problem from the other end?

What if, instead of seeking solace in prescription drugs, seeing shrink after shrink, or even doing affirmations until we're blue in the face, we addressed how we feel with our **voice**?

Here's an example of reversing cause and effect:

When patients with depression—for whom neither anti-depressants nor counseling had been working—were simply asked to smile, their mood improved, and it was much more difficult for them to stay feeling down. Their brains were receiving the message of happiness, and their brain chemistry and thoughts adjusted accordingly. It was, quite literally, almost impossible for them to feel down any longer. Bingo: a way for them to start to be happy, even if temporarily.

Repetition breeds habits. Good habits breed success. You can *start* with your body. When something is manifest in your body, it has a greater effect in reality than if something's just in your head.

That's why it's so important that we put our attention on what we want, instead of what we don't want, since we will manifest it into our body over time. (Here's where those affirmations come in handy, except they only tackle part of the problem.)

Put out a certain energy often enough, and it will manifest in your body. Thoughts and feelings have an energy which over time slows down in frequency, and becomes physical matter. Once something is matter, it's more manifest than a mere idea.

Therefore, when you deal directly with your breath, body, and voice—creating feelings and sensations in your body via your own frequencies—you can affect matter and everything else about your life.

SING YOURSELF WELL™ IN 7 SECONDS

The whole Universe is made of energy, of frequencies, and we literally have a built-in instrument that creates frequencies right in the middle of our bodies!

So: if you want to feel better and be happier, learn these steps to enliven your voice, and really master them. Then soon you can effortlessly do them any time you want, and within 7 seconds you'll feel better, every time.

Sing Yourself Well™ (SYW), gives you a shortcut to feeling great and being happy, snapping you out of pretty much any funk you might find yourself in. You can order the accompanying full course online at SingYourselfWell.com. You may also opt for the complete SYW system, which includes the online video training, and a personal in depth session.

I'm excited to start this journey with you, and want to congratulate you on taking this big, first, happy step in the direction of singing yourself well.

Happy healing!

CHAPTER 2

How to Get the Most out of This Book

1) You've already accomplished the most important part, because you're here and you're holding this guidebook in your hands! Yay!

Clearly, if you're reading this, you want to improve your health, vitality, and happiness. For this I congratulate you. You've accomplished step one, the most important step to effect change in your life. Kudos!

Let me tell you, had I had this book and training 30 years ago, I could have saved myself a whole lot of tears, fears, heartache, and pain. I wish from the bottom of my heart that the content of this book, along with the video training, brings you relief and joy, gives you energy, and tunes you in to the amazing, magical power that's already sitting within you, untapped: **your own voice**. Get ready!

2) Before you jump into the exercises in Part 2, read Part 1! Please :) Then, if you want to, finish with the bonuses in Part 3.

(Unless you are in a super duper hurry, then by all means jump to Part 2 right away. But I don't recommend it.)

I say this because reading the first part of the book will motivate you even further. The more motivated you are to get healthier, and happier, the more eager you'll be to actually do something about it. Makes sense, right? Plus, you'll gain a holistic understanding of what you're about to learn and experience. Think about it like taking a plane to fly over the land before you actually walk the grounds: it gives you perspective.

3) Read and follow the easy, yet profound exercises in Part 2 (and 3).

Not everyone learns by reading something. I know I have a hard time reading for extended periods of time (even if the book is my own!) That's why I made the accompanying **Sing Yourself Well** video training for you.

In the video course you'll be able to **see** and **hear** me demonstrate each exercise. You can stop, rewind, and later on, when reviewing, jump to the part you want to see and hear again. If you're anything like me, this way of learning will be more effective. Your eyes will see, your ears will hear, and your whole body will more effortlessly feel, or "get" how to "be". **Remember**: I had no clue how to sing holistically. I only knew that if I wanted to heal—which I desperately did—I had to figure stuff out. Fast.

When I finally really learned to sing, 1/3 of it was accomplished by taking lessons and practicing, but about 2/3 of it came through **watching and listening** to hundreds of sopranos. The more I watched and listened, the more my body understood what they, and especially what their bodies were doing to produce the desired sounds. So, go ahead and download the course to accompany the most important instructional part of the book. You'll be glad you did. (All of the videos are available for download on <u>SingYourselfWell.com</u>)

One last word: (Well, not really, but at least for now.)

When you buy a new toothbrush, you don't just put it on your shelf, hoping it'll somehow get your teeth clean. If you want results, you have to actually use it, right?

It's the same with the content of this book. It's one thing to understand why our culture is the way it is, why depression and anxiety are rampant in our time, why you often feel down and get sick as often as you do, and why and even how your voice can come to your rescue.

Yet it's a totally different thing to then roll up your sleeves and say "Well, I'm going to do something about it! I may not always feel like it, but I can totally spare a few seconds per day!" If you want change, you've got to enact that change.

The best news, however, is that I've made it super easy for you. It will—really—only take you seven seconds! This is what I want to encourage you to do: learn the system, practice it, and then make it a part of your daily routine.

CHAPTER 3

Who Should Read This? This is for You, If...

This book is for you, if you have a desire to get healthier and happier—it's as simple as that. There are, however, a few telltale signs that might indicate if this book is *especially* suited for you.

You can consider yourself a part of the voice healing VIPs, if you... (Take a deep breath)

- Are an introvert—Yay, go you!
- Get sick far too often.
- Are going through a "medium-size humdinger" of a life crisis.
- Are healing from an illness.
- Are so tired of feeling tired.
- Need a major, natural, energy booster.
- Find yourself repeating the same unhealthy relationship patterns
- Are the overworked and underappreciated parents of school-age kids.
- Have the mixed blessing of being in charge of lovely, yet "transformational" teens.
- Are the, and I mean, **the** voice of your business.

So, chances are, you've identified yourself in one—or all—of these categories. (I've found that most people who come to me will check off at least two or three of those "boxes.") Congratulations, you're ready to begin!

Now, I am urging you—pleading with you—to:

a) Read the book, (duh) Part 1.

b) Learn the voice tools in Part 2, and the bonuses in Part 3.

c) Ideally get the corresponding video training, so you can watch and hear me demonstrate the techniques while you do them along with me. This makes the entire process even easier, particularly if you are someone who learns best through visual and auditory media.

Once you've done all this, there is still one more crucial and often overlooked—or perhaps conveniently ignored—task:

Do it.

Do it every day, or at least most days. (No pressure, I'm not perfect, either.) Remember, we're talking about a mere 7 seconds a few times a day! That's all.

Practice this simple sequence...

- As a routine to get you going in the morning and make you feel clear and energized enough to tackle the day ahead.

- When you hit a speed bump, emotional or otherwise, during the day.

- To center yourself before a meeting, if you're feeling anxious.

- To clear out your sinuses, strengthen your lungs and immune system.

- To feel free, and to empower yourself.

Pretend it's your cup of coffee or espresso. Well, maybe do it *in addition* to having your morning cup of Joe. :) (Although there's a good chance you might not even need the caffeine afterwards.)

Seriously, it works that well.

This is for You if you're an Introvert

The danger we face. And how to bridge the gap happily!

So, my fellow introverts, if you're at all like me you probably…

- Love to read, paint, cook, garden, be quiet, or simply patter around your place, blissfully unconcerned with fulfilling any social responsibility, i.e. going to a party (shudder).

- Hate it when people call, or when you have to call someone, and they answer, and you actually are forced to talk to them.

- Find being around a lot of people incredibly draining.

- Feel that if another person addresses you with: "How-are-you?" and "Isn't-this-weather/band/movie-great?" and "What-have-you-been-up-to?" you might actually, finally, scream.

- Think theater audience participation was invented by the devil, or a particularly evil sorcerer.

On the upside, however…

- You have a keen sense of and attention to detail.

- You're highly tuned in and sensitive to your own feelings and those of others, whether they're expressed or not.

- Your creativity meter is off the charts.

- Your "BS detector" is highly acute, and doesn't come equipped with an off button. Ever.

- You've been called an "old soul" ever since you can remember.

If you nod—or even smirk—then yay! Chances are you, like me, are an introvert.

For decades I couldn't figure out what was "wrong" with me. As a little girl, I got bullied, stalked, and made fun of. People—teachers, parents, friends—were forever talking to me, wanting me to participate, trying to "draw me out" and "get me out of my own way." As a shy, quiet, and often scared young girl, these tactics only served to isolate me further (I went to exactly two parties in my teens—both a total nightmare). But the strange thing was that I only felt this way when other people were around. Once I was out in nature or alone at home I felt happy, cozy, free, and "myself." I could breathe, think, feel, and do what I needed in order to be happy.

So, when most of your friends go to parties, play entertaining but seemingly cruel pranks on one another, and excel in sports, and all you want to do is hide in your room, read, and pet your cat, it can feel like no one in the world understands who you are.

And they might not.

But **you do**, and that's the most important thing.

The world needs us introverts! Many of the world's greatest artists, thinkers, musicians, singers, composers, architects, and writers were—and are—introverts!

On the other hand we have extroverts. Extroverts easily express themselves throughout their lives. It makes them come across as social, jovial, charismatic, and as a result of this they often enjoy a great amount of freedom and power. By the way, even extroverts, at the end of the day, can feel incomplete because they may lack the introspective abilities the shyer segment of the population possess.

Therefore if you know an extrovert in need of some recharging or grounding, please have her or him read this as well!

But back to you. Here is our challenge as introverts: How far is going too far, and *exclusively, inward*?

How do we balance our inward tendencies with a physical, yet holistic form of self-expression, so our health and emotional wellbeing don't suffer? Without having to actually go anywhere, be around anyone?

You guessed it: you're holding the answer in your hands. The system you'll learn in part two takes care of that for you. You may never want to be on stage, or sing for other people at a party, and you don't have to (although once liberated, I couldn't keep myself away from performing). The thing is, once you've got the sequence down, every time you practice it, you'll feel as if you could do just that—as if you were as strong and grounded as a redwood tree.

You'll get, within a few seconds, the energy an extrovert naturally feels, all while remaining in the comfort of your home, without ever having to encounter another human being—well, except me, in your videos. Then, with this new energy available to you at any time, you can be a more fully realized version of your already extraordinary self.

This is for You if Your Want Better Health and More Energy

Read the signs and take action!

- Do you often feel depressed or anxious?
- Do you tend to have low energy and feel tired a lot more than you should?
- Does it seem as if you're getting sick way more than others?

- Are you healing from an illness, and are in need of an extra boost?
- Do you suffer from allergies or shortness of breath?
- Do you tend to experience the same unhealthy patterns in your relationships?
- Do you feel shy and want more confidence?

If you can identify with any of these, take heart. I know you have most likely tried so many approaches to healing yourself. Some worked for a while, and some others just didn't. These conditions can be debilitating to the point where you almost feel as if you must accept the fact that they're a part of you, and that you'll never be able to clear that layer of fog from your head or body.

I did, too!

Until my crisis, I didn't really think there was anything I could change about the way my body was, or the way I felt about it. Well, my dear, when your body experiences the freedom you're about to experience, then you might find it's able to let go of so many more of those old patterns you once thought were a permanent part of you.

Among the hundreds of students I've had, there have been many who came to me with some physical manifestation of an imbalance. But after following this organic sequence of steps only a few times, and then continuing at home, their symptoms all but vanished!

So whether you get colds a lot, or never really feel energized, or have been diagnosed with a weak immune system, take heart, and express your voice. Fully!

Energizing your body the right way is a vital step in enabling you to feel happier and healthier, and I've developed the Sing Yourself Well™ program to do just that.

This is for You if You're the Overworked and Underappreciated Parent of School Age Kids or Teens

Is this You?

- You worry about your kids getting bullied, or bullying others.

- You worry about them being healthy and happy.

- You want your kids to *feel* and *do* what's right for them.

- You want to be a loving, patient, clear, parent who has the respect of your kids.

- You want to acknowledge and fulfill *your own* needs.

- You want to stay connected with your kids throughout their teens.

- And yes, you might also want to retain at least some of your sanity.

Congratulations. These are wonderful—and, may I add, lofty—ambitions and desires. But the disconnect between expectations and reality is often much more pronounced than we would have hoped. It's natural to feel down on yourself sometimes if you feel unable to follow your ideals. As parents we know that more often than not we lose ourselves in our kids and their activities, all too easily.

Between running errands, signing a gazillion pieces of school papers, driving them to and picking them up from soccer, tennis, or ballet, packing a healthy, balanced lunch, listening to them tell you what's important in their lives, nagging them a dozen times to tidy their room, the demands on you—the human being—are sometimes quite overwhelming.

But where does time for **you** fit into all of that? As a parent, you need a quick, effortless, fun, and especially *effective* way to center yourself and your kids. There is of course, your meditation, which I strongly recommend, morning and evening to center and ground yourself.

But what about during the day?

Well, you most likely have seven seconds a few times per day, at the very least, don't you? Good, because that's all you need! The tools provided later in this book will give you a quick way to get centered in your own body whenever you feel as if you've been overextending, and doing too much for other people.

And please, once you've learned the tools, feel free to teach them to your children as well! Just like it does for you, it can help them feel more comfortable to be themselves, and make the best possible choices for their own lives.

Here's a free Kids' ebook you can read with them, so they can learn from you and the book: singyourselfwell.com/free-kids-ebook/

Best-selling author Jack Canfield also said this about the 7 Second Reset™: "This is something parents can teach their kids, so kids can change their state!"

This is for You if you're the Voice of Your Business

This is for You, my fellow solo-entrepreneur!

- Do you own a business—either established or start-up?
- Does the thought of speaking in front of a hall full of potential clients get you happy and excited, or rather nervous and anxious?

- When you do a webinar, video, or in person meeting, does your heart beat out of your chest, causing you to feel insecure and nervous?

- Do you hate the sound of your voice?

- Do you get hoarse, or a sore throat when talking for a long time?

- Have you done the mind set thing, the inner game thing, and you *still* feel insecure or unsure of your mission, message or self worth?

- Would you love a *natural* boost of confidence whenever you need it?

Consider this:

Your voice—the way you sound—is *crucially important* to your success both in life and in business. In the midst of all the hype about the visual medium being the thing to worry about in this visual culture, somehow the importance of audio in regards to how information is transmitted and received got lost.

Let me ask you this:

How many times have you listened to a webinar or podcast, where you didn't have a visual of the person talking? And how many times of those have you suddenly closed the page, and "clicked away," either right away or midway through? I know I have. There were times when I liked the person, and really needed what she or he had to offer, but then this uneasy feeling began growing in my body. As I listened to their voice I experienced more and more "internal wincing," as I call it, until I finally decided to close the window, breathing, often, a sigh of relief.

Now that's not a good sign for anyone, least of all aspiring entrepreneurs!

I don't want this to happen to you and your business. You could potentially lose hundreds of clients, and hundreds of thousands of dollars.

Instead, I want you to feel, and as a result, be received and perceived as sublimely confident and at ease. You might already feel this way, say, when you're relaxing at home or in your favorite coffee shop, talking to a close friend about your business. In these situations you're probably fairly confident, right? When you work on your business or even talk about it to friends, you become enthusiastic, and can't wait to get out there and reach tons of people, right?

So why is it then that, when your favorite coffee house becomes a conference hall and your friend becomes a group of potential clients, you jump out of your own skin with fear or intimidation, afraid of being judged? What is it that suddenly happens—where your throat tightens, your mouth feels parched, your breath jumps high up into your chest, and your voice cracks?

Somewhere along the line you left your body and got into your head.

Fear, intimidation, anxiety—whatever you want to call it—took over and rattled you to the point where you couldn't relax, act natural, and *perform*.

It's now more crucial than ever to go back to the basics:

- **Be connected** to both the Divine *and* your body no matter the situation.
- **Trust** in your unique mission.
- **Use your body** as the tool to anchor yourself, with the help of your breath and voice.
- **Express** who you are and what you are here to do with your voice in a powerful, effortless way.

When you have this sequence at your disposal, you'll find that you can pop into your center anytime, give your body and mind a boost, and feel your real, authentic confidence and power within 7 seconds.

That way, the only responses you'll ever get are those from loyal customers, and the only "click" you'll hear is from clients enthusiastically signing up for what you have to offer!

(Stay tuned for the release of **"Your Irresistible Voice"**, written with the vocal professional and solo entrepreneur in mind.)

CHAPTER 4

When and How It All Happened: My Sing Yourself Well Story

Do you know the feeling when you discover something great, and you just can't keep quiet about it, you're so excited?

Well, the book you're holding in your hands does that for me! I just couldn't contain it within myself any longer. It was pushing from the inside to come out, like a baby. Even if none of it had ever made me a penny, I passionately want every woman, man and child to know these secrets.

Over the years I've noticed there seem to be two types of (mostly) women who seek my help:

On the one hand, spiritual women who are dealing with midlife crises, relationship problems, parenting issues, or health problems.

And while each case is different in its own way, I find that in almost all cases there exists a common theme: all of the women are, in one way or another, without being aware of it, desperately in need to open up their voice, and integrate it with their breath and their true, spiritual nature.

Most of all: They all have the need to express themselves!

Then there are—mostly younger—voice students who come to me because they feel they want to learn how to improve their singing (or even learn how to sing in the first place).

And in almost all cases they need—in addition to voice lessons—a holistic, energetic clearing and healing of their whole person, before any of the other work can be really effective. Be it parent-child issues, sibling issues or school/career related issues, they're eager to grow beyond those, and get to where they're able to truly shine as the young adults they're becoming. **They all need holistic, energetic support.**

Now here's the most interesting part:

You know how business people and entrepreneurs do research, and ask questions in order to find out what people want and need, before they "market" to them?

Well, over the years I've consulted hundreds of clients, tuned into them energetically, and yes, asked some questions, too. But mostly, it was my intuition that picked up on their needs.

Here are the results:

Every single woman needed to implement the same 7 changes in her life, relating to her energy, body, breath, and voice!

These **7 needs** involved: 1) Becoming aware of themselves, and their own needs (sound familiar?). 2) Relaxing, taking every moment as it comes. 3) Figuring out who they are and what they're here to experience, in short, aligning themselves with their Higher purpose. 4) Being open to, and at ease with whatever is. 5) Improving flow of communication, within their own body, and between themselves and others. 6) Feeling more empowered and strong. 7) Finally, having more energy, not getting so tired, feeling lively and alert.

This is what turned into the **7 qualities** every woman (man and child) needs in order to be happy, balanced, and healthy: awareness, relaxation, alignment, openness, flow, power, and energy.

I'm describing them in more detail in their own chapter (Chapter 8), and the 7 steps are the physical instruction on how to make these qualities manifest in your body as fast as possible.

Over the past 17 years what has evolved from these observations is a very organic and highly effective method that combines energetic healing with vocal training. What you're getting here is the easy, holistic, and effective system that is now available in its most complete form.

Hundreds of women have now tested and grown from these simple yet profound holistic tools. These women come from a range of backgrounds—professional singers, yoga instructors, entrepreneurs, students, and full time moms.

Their prior exposure to spirituality and healing varies greatly from person to person, but in each case the results are the same: after going through the simple steps I'll be outlining for you in this book, all of these women leave feeling reinvigorated, more powerful, and free.

And it's so easy.

The best part of it all, in fact, is that you, dear reader, already possess the tools necessary to complete these incredible transformations. You just need to learn how to use them for maximum effect on your wellbeing.

And here is what lead to it all.......

My Personal Story:

I am living proof that shutting yourself up and closing yourself off to the world is not what you should be doing. Ever.

If you, like me, were born into a family of four generations of musicians and singers—your mom, alone, was a teacher, conductor, and singer—you might think that this set you up for a lifelong love of all things vocal, musical and rhythmical.

For me, it did—and it didn't.

I was a shy, introverted four year old when my mother brought home a 3-LP set of Mozart's *The Magic Flute*. After unwrapping the sleeve and poring over the pictures, I crouched on the floor, ears to the speakers, transfixed, for hours.

Within a few days I had practically memorized the whole score. I could sing along to the Queen of the Night's famously elaborate and high-pitched aria as if it were a lullaby. I loved it.

Later on, I sang in my mom's school choir and played piano concertos with her orchestra. Those outlets, along with ballet, ice dancing, tennis, and horseback riding were great ways to balance my otherwise shy, introverted nature.

So, you'd think I was well on my way to becoming a professional singer, or music teacher. Well, the answer is yes, but also a resounding no!

Something else had happened when I was a child, which ran parallel to my musical endeavors:

When I was five years old, I drowned.

I was playing badminton at my girlfriend's house. Running backwards to catch the bird, I tripped over the edge of their small, deep pool, and fell in.

Within a second I was submerged in the water, felt disoriented, and had no idea whether I was swimming up or down. I kicked and struggled to get back "up" to the surface, but instead just seemed to go further and further down.

Within a few moments I was breathing water. It didn't hurt, but I quickly panicked, as I could feel how my lungs were filling with water. My body was getting weaker and weaker, and finally shut down.

A "movie reel" with an amazingly accurate and detailed clip after clip of my life's experiences swiftly scrolled down before my inner eye, making me recap each and every experience of my short life—and then...

Something extraordinary happened that was the lighthouse, or corner stone for the rest of my life:

I "woke up."

It was as if so far I had been sleeping or dreaming, and only now, **without my body, was I fully awake**.

I felt as if I was home. Really, truly, fully home. As if I had never been anywhere else.

Nothing to worry about, nothing to fight for, nothing to be afraid of.

I felt one with all there was, is, and ever will be. A soft, glistening light emanated from within myself and everything else. As a matter of fact, everything was light—made of light—surrounded by light—creating light. Alongside it there was a beautiful, peaceful feeling and sound, of comfort, clarity, ease, beauty, and wisdom.

The feeling of peace, happiness, clarity, ease, and perfection can only be described with the feeling of being at home, where everything is so familiar, you don't even realize where you are.

—What a total shock it was, then, when suddenly I could feel it ending, and feel myself getting pulled back into my body.

My girlfriend, as I found out later, had run off to fetch her mother, who fished my lifeless body out of the water. I awoke wrapped in thick, gray, wool blankets, looking up at their worried faces.

Of course they were worried sick, feeling relief only when I opened my eyes after what to them, seemed to have been an eternity.

To me, however, the experience had been such a different one.

It was coming back to the body, which seemed like an incomprehensible letdown!

I had just entered a sparkling, light-filled, humming celestial realm—a realm which was actually me, my own inner nature. I had felt a sense of oneness, wholeness, a sense of "being home" in a glistening, humming pool of universal love and creation, where everything moved at a pace and according to an order that was seemingly beyond any human control or intellectual comprehension.

There is no other way to describe it than to say that it was absolutely Divine. There was nothing to wish for, nothing to worry about—just bliss. What struck me the most was how familiar this realm felt. It felt, literally, again, like *coming home*.

You can see why I was quite dismayed, when it turned out I had to return to my body and pick up where I left off.

Although it wasn't *exactly* where I had left off, because this experience never left me completely. For the rest of my childhood, teenage, and adult years I yearned for it to become permanent.

Being a spiritual introvert, it was really tough to be around so many other people all the time—in school, athletics, all the various social activities my parents organized for me, and even the more casual situations with friends. I desperately missed the oneness I had experienced when I was temporarily without my body.

Enter: the unexpected relief I found when I turned 20, and a friend introduced me to the Transcendental Meditation (TM) technique.

I was, like so many others still are, skeptical at first. Remember: I grew up in post-war Germany where it had been drummed into all of our heads to never, ever follow a leader (or guru) ever again. Not even someone benevolent and enlightened who gives hope to the world teaching a simple meditation technique.

And yet here I was, about to do just that.

Reluctantly, I sat down for my first meditation, squirming, and almost having second thoughts. When suddenly, after just about 15 seconds, by following the simple instructions... there it was again, finally: That familiar, blissful feeling I had been waiting for, for so long!

Tears were streaming down my cheeks when I realized I was in the state I had missed so much, and longed for so deeply all these years: I felt once again, I had found *home*! Just like when I was five and had drowned.

I didn't know it, but I had waited for the experience of meditation since I was a little girl spending countless hours sitting in meadows, communing in my own way with wildflowers, insects, animals, trees, the wind, clouds, and the sky.

So when I found meditation—or rather, when it found me—and I sat down to meditate, I was home again, back in the place I had glimpsed when I was young and so near death. In that meditation room, tears running down my cheeks, I knew that all was well, and I would be all right.

But, as life would have it, I wasn't done learning yet.

With all of the time spent meditating and focusing on my inner life, including spending two and a half sublime years around Maharishi, and later becoming a teacher of TM—I had totally forgotten the other crucial part of life: to express myself on the outside. I had neglected my outward "dharma" or destiny —the one my family had given me, of being a musician, singer, artist and performer.

To play catch up: at age 18 I had auditioned with the esteemed head of the famous voice and music conservatory in Munich. When I wanted to sing the aria I had prepared in the higher range I was comfortable in, the professor had me forgo the song, and instead sing a simple scale in the middle range, in which I sucked. Sure enough, after a few notes, she interrupted me, hitting her fingers on the keys, and sent me home, saying I wasn't ready, or good enough, and that it was *too late for me to become a singer*. Too late? I was 18!

Needless to say, I was crushed.

I know now that it just wasn't the time for me to become a performer. I was way too introverted to sustain any kind of touring and late-night performing schedule. So it was just as well it didn't work out.

But, sadly, the experience was traumatizing enough to make me stop singing and expressing myself all together.

That is, at least, until my terrifying wake-up call that came over a decade later.

SING YOURSELF WELL™ IN 7 SECONDS

One blizzardy winter evening when I was 32, I found myself standing in Dr. Deepak Chopra's practice near Boston, where—after I had reached out and alerted him of my feared condition—he was gracious enough to see me. After he examined me in his office, he told me something I'll never forget:

Ulrike, you have thyroid cancer. This is an imbalance of the throat chakra, the center of self expression. I've known you for many years, and you never say anything. Now your throat chakra is blocked, because you've not been expressing yourself. To heal, you have to speak up, sing, and express yourself.

I was stunned, shocked, and terribly frightened. Yet I felt strangely relieved, too, as now I knew *why* this had happened to me.

As a lifelong introvert—and at this point, a longtime meditator, and meditation teacher—I hadn't even thought about the need to express myself since childhood! Much less had I done anything about it.

Up until that point, no other doctor had been so right on *why* I had developed this disease.

When I had seen a conventional specialist earlier that year, the experience was entirely different. That enormously overweight doctor huffed and puffed into the room, ruler in hand, and without even looking into my eyes, saying hello, or shaking my hand, he came up to my throat, held the ruler next to the growth, and told its exact measurements to his assistant. He then told me "we'll have to cut the whole thing out."

I was stone-cold with fear. There was no relief at all. No insight, no reason why, just hard, material, physical facts.

When, however, I heard Dr. Chopra's compassionate, holistic explanation, I felt—despite having received what was essentially the same diagnosis—a strange sense of relief. After alerting me of what he believed to have been the cause for my cancer, Dr. Chopra got practical. He got on the phone and called the renowned Dr. Wang, an elderly Chinese surgeon. Alas, Dr. Wang told him he was going to retire the day after tomorrow (terrible timing) and that he had no openings to see me. My heart sank.

Miraculously, however, when I got to my hotel in Boston after returning from the appointment, I was greeted by a red flashing light on the room's answering machine. I listened to the message: it was from the hospital. Unbelievably enough, Dr. Wang had had a cancellation, and he was wondering if I could come in for surgery the next morning at 7 a.m.!

I fell to my knees in tears and gratitude, for this amazing wave of nature support, and for Dr. Chopra's insight, kindness, love, and hurried, practical action. Without him I may never have known that I *needed to sing to heal* myself!

As soon as I was able, I followed his advice: Within a few weeks and in the coming years I learned arias (operatic songs), took notes, reviewed voice lessons my mother had sent me from Germany, and listened to and observed as many female opera singers as possible.

Interestingly, the arias I was most attracted to were from the opera "Carmen" by Bizet. For some reason the passionate nature of the female character, and the way it was expressed in her rhythmical arias really appealed to me.

For a long time my "warm ups" would simply consist of singing her arias over and over again.

When teaching, I often use one of Carmen's arias to work with clients, as it lends itself beautifully to establishing flow in their voice.

At my very first house concert for friends, naturally, I sang these arias. To this day I love singing them, because they make me feel free, grounded, powerful, and happy.

As the introvert I am, Carmen is way too much to live in daily life. But for those minutes and hours in the day when I need this outlet, it's perfect.

Now, and for the past 25 years, and especially since taking official lessons at age 40, I've been singing and performing as often as I can, accompanied both by piano when performing in smaller spaces, and by orchestra when singing in larger venues.

I cannot even begin to tell you the joy and thrill I experience when I sing and perform. When I sing with my full breath and power, it's almost like flying—weightless, invincible, and free. I so want that for you, too!

In the past 17 years I've also taught hundreds of spiritually-inclined female clients and students, non-singers and singers alike, how to express themselves, in order to increase their health, success, relationships, and overall wellbeing.

The book you're reading is the first, and most basic of seven books in the works. Each of them will address a specific area of concern, and how you can profoundly transform your life with the power of your voice.

We all need the healing power of our voice, because of its holistic importance of self expression for our health and happiness.

I wouldn't wish these wake-up calls on you or anyone, so please, read on!

CHAPTER 5

Why We Don't Sing

A word about our culture and its influence on your voice

There are several reasons why we stop using our full voice.

- Upbringing/Education
- Culture
- History of Government
- History of Religion
- Medical Establishment
- Entertainment/Celebrity Worship
- "You"

But, despite how the presence of that last point might make it seem (I'll get to it), none of it is your fault! For starters, no one teaches us this way of using our full voice when we're young. But why is that? Wouldn't it be in society's best interest if everybody was using their full voice, inside and out?

If we're comfortable with our voice, inner and outer, it means we know who we are inside, and we're not afraid to express this on the outside. Does this sound good to you? Yes? It does to me, too! But, now, can you think of a few people or institutions who might not exactly applaud you for that? Let's look at a few areas of our culture which, in the past, had a great interest in keeping you conveniently silent, or small.

First, there's our **upbringing**. Especially if we're of a certain generation we were often told early on to be quiet and not interrupt the adults while they're talking—or else there'd be hell to pay.

When or if we attempted to sing our hearts out, we may have heard another kind of criticism: "You sing off key;" "Too loud;" "You can't carry a tune;" "Your voice isn't very pretty." As a result, many of us shut ourselves up for good. What effect does this have? When we don't use our full voices our health suffers, our longevity is lessened, and we're more prone to depression, anxiety, and a host of other culturally inflicted imbalances.

Sometime between childhood and adulthood, most of us stop expressing ourselves. We stop speaking our truth, stop playing, and stop singing freely just for the joy of it.

Research (at the University of California, Oxford University Press, and the National Center for Biotechnology) shows that the transition from childhood to adulthood often leads to a decrease in free self-expression, and this can have serious consequences for our mental, emotional, and physical health.

Shouldn't our self-expression actually grow as we get older?

Traditionally our voice has been seen as a tool for communicating with others, for pleasing others, or worse, for being criticized by others. We thought our voice belonged to others.

But in reality, our voice is actually our own healing tool! After all, it's in our own body, right?

In addition, when you have people who don't voice their own opinion, you have a **culture of conformity**. The "convenient" result is that complacency increases, making for a more easily governable society. Historically, people in society who spoke up against the incumbent authority were not rewarded. Instead, outspoken people were often persecuted. Even today, our nation claims to advocate the right to free speech. But in reality, through a complex system of cultural conditioning, we're being told what to think, how to act, and what not to do almost constantly.

The second reason for this culture of silence, tied to our upbringing, is the nature of our **education**. Over the last few decades we've seen a massive decrease of music and choir classes being offered in schools. Instead, more and more emphasis has been placed on teaching young students "practical" skills, such as math or writing.

As a result of these changes, however, children are less and less able to feel inwardly who they are, and outwardly, how to express themselves creatively with their full body and full voice. This poses some inherent problems, especially when you consider that the creative impulse is at the very basis of our existence!

After all, Creation comes first, then all the knowledge about it. Our very bodies are *created* first, before we learn to talk, walk and learn. Giving children back their voices, and educating them how to use them the right way, inside and out, will enact fundamental changes in their lives.

Children who sing—and speak—with their full voice are able to be more in tune with who they are, and what is good for them, rather than being bullied into doing what others want for them. Tied to this is an increased sense of self-worth, and an ability to become resilient to the influences of the media.

Of course, another fundamental benefit of teaching children to sing from an early age is that the act of singing itself will keep kids healthier than they've ever been before, as their bodies—courtesy of a boosted immune system—learn to fend off viruses and infections.

The next factor that serves to stifle our voices is something I touched on briefly in the previous section: the **government**. Looking at many of the governments in American history and the history of other countries, you'll observe that they very rarely encouraged people to speak out and speak up.

Why is that?

Simple: Ultimately it isn't very convenient for the ruler of a country to have his or her people think for themselves and voice their opinions. Why would you want a free person, when that person is much harder to control?

Yet, if we're in touch with our full voice, who we are and want to be, guess what would happen? We would have a more balanced society; a happier one in which each person is uniquely her/himself, secure in her/himself and contributing exactly what each one is meant to contribute, each according to her/his destiny and skills.

Ruling from fear has no future—not in this day and age. We've come too far. So many of us have been meditating for a long time, are seekers, and living a conscious life. The health of our bodies, our kids and the earth is at stake, and it's time we wake up and take control over our voice as well.

This brings me to the next factor that has served to stifle our voices throughout history: **religion**. "Religio" means source in Latin, so really it refers to our very nature of oneness with the Divine.

However, we've observed that, throughout history, various (not all) religions have instructed their followers that the path to God is only available through their specific means and methods. After all, there's no business in making people aware that each of us has a direct wire to God available at all times.

Trust me: In the long run, it's easier, more effective, more compassionate, more guilt-free, and less expensive to have your own, direct dialogue with God, Source, Divine, your Self, or whatever it is for you.

For me, the most direct path to my Self has been TM (Transcendental Meditation) for the past many decades, but it will inevitably differ for each individual and their unique experience. Once you've had this experience of transcending, you will know where you "live"—where your true self resides—and no religion can ever take it away. They can just add to it beautifully, if that's what you desire.

Then, once you've found this channel of connecting to your inner Self, come out and express that "new you" to the world—fully, without holding back.

The tools in this book were designed to help you do just that: They give you the direct experience of being centered in your own body, breath, voice, and self in an effortless way, and then to come out and express who you are to the world. Being centered in your own body, any time you want to, is the best way to connect with Divine in an immediate way.

The next factor in society that has conditioned this culture of silence is the **medical establishment**. Commonly termed "big pharma," the medical establishment deals in the business of illness, disease and decay. The more enlightened practitioners, of course, would love to see everyone healthy, but there's still an insidious monetary interest that overwhelms much of this initial good will.

Why would you want people to be healthy, when you can sell and feed them pills that have side effects, and then sell them pills to counteract those side effects? It's not in big pharma's interest to have people a) be healthy and b) find a cure for their illness that works for them, outside of the pharmaceutical industry.

When you empower yourself through your full voice and breath, however, you know your body better, and are aware of when it might be imbalanced; plus you'll have a direct means to provide it with extra strength.

One of the last and most important reasons we don't express ourselves is that, quite plainly, we don't see it to be our "place." We'd rather safely watch as someone else lives our dream as performer, living vicariously through others, as they say.

Thing is, we were all born with a unique voice, and the inherent anatomical ability to sing. Sadly, as we graduate from child to teen to young adult, many of us get more self-conscious, and we can't help but compare ourselves to other, younger, "cooler," more successful people.

Soon, it seems as if we divide ourselves into two categories: those who follow their dharma/destiny and express themselves, and those who simply listen passively, at best trying to imitate—in other words: those who sing, and those who don't.

Our current **celebrity culture** which has grown so rapidly over the last decades has caused us to worship celebrities and performers, rather than create music and sing on our own. Comparing ourselves to those impossible ideals makes us shrink back into ourselves and shut ourselves up. Then, when we do sing, we do so with headphones, plugged in, trying to sound like the singer we listen to, entirely unaware of our own voice, of what we actually sound like.

Your body was born free and unique! When we model or compare ourselves, and adjust our voice to others, we're not free to sing how our body wants to express itself.

Also, as we age and become more self-aware, the pressure to 'fit in' increases. We compare ourselves, thinking "Oh, my voice isn't as pretty as hers," etc. The results are grim, and include stunted personal growth due to restricted creative expression, and a body that has shut down, and doesn't feel free or empowered.

This brings us to the last, and trickiest, reason you don't sing like you could: "**You.**" You don't mean to, and it's not your fault, but "you" are, in fact, at times, your own worst critic. The reason the "you" is in quotes, however, is that this is not the real you!

The "you" that judges is the product of accumulated and unaddressed stresses from the past. The *real* you is underneath, **waiting to come out and play**, but until that happens, it's incredibly important not to let the fake "you" judge the *real you*.

Now, a brief note regarding **judgment**:

We judge *others* all the time, because in them we see something that we perceive as an imperfection. But wouldn't it be easier if we simply accepted what is, and how people are? (Good luck! I know…)

We judge *ourselves* because we want to be loved; because love resonates the most with who we really are.

You can see even with these factors alone how easy it is to shut up, feel discouraged, and never even consider using our voice.

Well, let's change all of that. Today, let's take a bold stand. Today, commit you'll read this book, and learn the seven simple steps that will enable you to take back your health and happiness.

After all, do you not have the right to express yourself? Of course you do! You're a Divine Being here on earth solely for the purpose of expressing yourself! Whether you're an introvert or extrovert, a little bit of both (an "ambivert"), or something entirely different, you deserve to be *you*—the real you, who is healthy, happy, fulfilled, free, strong, and loved.

You owe it to yourself to go all-out in being who you wanted to be before you came into this life.

So be it. Do it. Now.

It's time.

CHAPTER 6

Why We Need to Sing - Your Voice Shapes Your and Our World

The shocking truth about our full potential

Did you know that we use just about **20%** of our voice in daily life? On an average day, the average person speaks using a range that is less than a fifth of an octave, especially when feeling down!

When sitting and talking with my clients, usually before they took lessons, I couldn't help but notice the notes between which their speaking voice moved. Each time I became aware, I went over to the piano and, time after time, the average range of notes they used for speaking was about 5/8s of an octave, or 5-8 notes in the chromatic scale.

Now, maybe you're not aware, but the average range of a human voice encompasses about 40 notes. 40. Not 5-8:

- Speaking voice range:

The average human speaking voice range covers about 1/3 to 1/2 of an octave, 5-8 notes.

- Singing voice range:

The average human singing voice range is typically about 3 1/3 octaves, with many people having a range even larger than that, according to Sloan School of Music. This translates to approximately 40 notes a person can vocalize.

Do you know how crazy it is to voluntarily only use 20% of your voice, shutting yourself off to 80% of your vocal potential? And did you know that we only use about 20% of our lung capacity as well? (Athletes use 50%, opera singers and brass players use 80%.)

So how can **you**—presumably not a professional opera singer, brass player, or athlete—get the benefits that people of those professions possess, without actually having to master that coloratura aria, the trumpet, or the high jump?

By now you *know* the answer: Over the last 25 years I've compiled the perfect solution, the Sing Yourself Well Signature System, specifically designed to accommodate non-singers who want the benefits that come with having the breath control and vocal potential of a professional singer.

Why would you voluntarily use only 20% of a precious faculty given to us *for free* by nature? One might say:

"Well, I'm not a singer, so why should I sing? I'm okay with just using 20% of my voice."

But do you want to know how crazy this would be? It's like saying:

"Well, I'm not an athlete, so why should I use my whole body? I'm okay with just using 20% of my body and hopping around on one leg for the rest of my life."

Crazy, right?

Or, say you own a house with five rooms, yet for some bizarre reason you choose to only live in the dining room, and you never even set foot in your kitchen, living room, bathroom or bedroom.

Equally crazy, right?

Yet this is how many of us feel about using our voice! What's the effect? We shut up and stifle our self-expression.

As we mentioned earlier, often in childhood we were told to "Be quiet;" or to "Use your inside voice." These demands often came alongside direct criticism such as "You sing off key;" "You can't carry a tune;" or "Your voice isn't very pretty." It's understandable, then, that so many of us shut ourselves up, sometimes for good. But did you know that by harnessing the full potential of your voice you literally have the power to change your body, health, mood, energy, and even life span?

Using your full voice is good for you emotionally, physically, spiritually, and socially: It's a great workout for your lungs, heart and circulation, helps to improve sleep, tone facial muscles (really, it's the cheapest facelift available), and beat depressive or anxious tendencies.

I've seen so many instances in which a client's voice was the **missing link** to their achieving fulfillment. I, too, have always found that when I don't sing I have low energy, get cranky, or even depressed. It turns out I was far from the only one. My students and healing voice clients, as well as singers and researchers all over the world have found the same to be true.

In a very real way, your voice influences your health, happiness, vitality, relationships, and overall well being. In that, your voice shapes your world.

Research over the past 8 years (from institutions like the University of Gothenburg, University College London, and Iowa State University) has shown that singing boosts our immune system, increases lung capacity, improves posture and confidence, and overall makes us happier.

Below I've outlined ten very practical reasons how using your full voice to sing with proper technique helps to increase your overall well being.

1. Singers have better posture and, accordingly, more **self-confidence**.

2. Singing releases endorphins which make you **happier**.

3. You naturally develop healthier breathing patterns. Your breath sits lower in your body when you sing properly, signaling an increased willingness to **relax** for your body and brain. *"Singing makes us breathe more deeply than many forms of strenuous exercise, so we take in more oxygen, improve aerobic capacity, and experience a **release of muscle tension** as well."* — Professor Graham Welch, Director of Educational Research, University of Surrey, UK

4. When you sing, your body releases oxytocin—a natural stress reliever—that helps **reduce depression**, low energy, hopelessness and loneliness. (*TIME magazine*)

5. Heart rate variability (HRV) is the natural variation in the time between your heartbeats, and is often used as a sign of how well your heart and nervous system are working together. In general, slow, steady breathing can raise HRV, and singing in a way that encourages this kind of calm, regular breathing can temporarily increase HRV.

6. Singers show lower levels of cortisol, (less* stress), which helps you **sleep better**.

7. Singing works your lungs, **improves circulation**, and **builds strength** in your abdominal and intercostals.

8. Singing with your full lung capacity strengthens your **immune system**, according to research by scientists at the University of Frankfurt in Germany, published in the *US Journal of Behavioral Medicine*.

9. Singing properly using all resonances **opens** up your **sinuses** and respiratory tract, often **alleviating breathing problems** and **allergies**.

10. Singing is good for your brain, enhances your mental awareness, and improves your **concentration** and **memory**.

With all these positive physiological and psychological changes, you may just end up living longer as a result of your practice.

Many opera singers (with good supportive technique) are able to perform on stage well into their 80's and live well above the average age for non-singers. For example: the Italian Soprano *Magda Olivero* sang her last concert at age 99, and lived until 104!

The good news is that even if singing is not your thing, simply using your **full** voice a few times a day will give you some of the same benefits these singers have spent most of their lives cultivating.

Part 2 of this book will show you how to quickly and easily learn to use your full voice in an effortless way. Once learned, you can start to reap the health benefits of an opera singer, in just a few seconds a few times a day.

But there's another reason why it's so timely and vital for you to sing and find your voice, inner and outer, and that is:

Your voice, on a subtle and powerful level—shapes our entire world!

You have most likely been aware for some time that we live in very interesting, dynamic times. The collective consciousness of our world is rapidly changing. So many of us have been seekers of truth, the deeper meaning of life, meditating for years or even decades—and it shows.

The world is waking up—waking up to a different way of functioning. Instead of predominately being ruled by the head—the mind and intellect—more and more of us have been listening to our hearts. A decision based on our hearts is hardly ever wrong. Honing our intuition to where we spontaneously distinguish right from wrong, and are able to feel out what's the right thing for us at any given moment, is something I encourage in myself and you, too.

Part of that waking up to a more heart-centered way of living has at its base a trend that has been slowly gathering momentum:

The rise of what is called "The Divine Feminine."

The term "Divine Feminine" often gets confused with something implying some form of feminism. Not that this is a bad thing in and of itself.

However, the Divine Feminine is more than that: We're all part of Divine. Divine is complete and therefore genderless. Once it manifests, it does so in its totality. Meaning, in order to compartmentalize and divide or polarize "Itself", it has to find a way to not lose its totality. Makes sense, right?

Enter: The Divine polarity—comprised of Divine Feminine, *and* Divine Masculine.

We all have both. Some of us have a really good balance of both. Some of us have one more than the other. It's all good. It's all part of the Divine plan.

We now happen to live in a time where an increase of the Divine Feminine is what the world needs.

The past many centuries, even millennia, were dominated by an abundance of the Divine masculine, as portrayed in male artists, warriors, athletes, writers, factory workers, mechanics, kings, architects, explorers, scientists, and religious and political leaders. We needed all of it.

Now we're seeing signs of the rise of the Divine Feminine, to bring balance into the world once again.

The Divine Feminine has its strengths in communication, artistic expression, self expression, compassion, nurturing, connecting, expressing affection, caring for animals, healing, collaboration, and intuition.

And yes, this can, and most likely will come in the form of women's strive for equal rights, of compassionate treatment of all people, no matter race, gender, or orientation, and artistic, as well as many other expressions.

But here's the interesting thing, which challenges what we might expect:

Rather than getting hung up on a certain gender exemplifying one flavor of Divine—as in the Divine Feminine being exemplified by women exclusively—it's quite common to have this quality being expressed and infused into the world by more and more men as well!

- That's why people like Bernie Sanders, Maharishi Mahesh Yogi, the Pope Francis, and some rap artists like Prince Ea are/were so successful.
- That's why men with the nurturing Divine Feminine tend to want to be stay-at-home dads, and the kids love it.
- That's why we're seeing an increase of earth-protecting environmental laws, sustainable agriculture, as well as the rise of solar and wind technologies.

All these are examples of the rise of the Divine Feminine.

For the Divine Feminine to be felt, heard, and expressed, we need to get very good at feeling who we are. We need to find our *inner voice*, be okay with it—instead of fighting it or looking to the outside to define us—and then express who we are to the world with our unique *outer voice*.

We need to heal the old ways of existing, and embrace the new, intuitive, heart-based way of *being* in the world. That can scare the bejesus out of some, for sure, but it's the only way forward.

Your unique, God-given voice is the key to not just your own life, but to the life of everyone around you, the life of our planet, and the whole universe. By learning to tune into your unique inner voice, and learning to express your full outer voice, you are *literally changing the frequencies of our entire world.*

I believe in women and men with a good portion of the Divine Feminine leading the way for the next little while.

And by "little while" I mean in the cosmic sense. It could really be thousands of years. :)

CHAPTER 7

Why We Breathe

Breath Comes First!

Any doubts? Try not breathing—and you'll quickly understand its importance when it comes to your health and happiness.

It seems obvious enough, right? Yet so many people aren't even conscious of the fact they're breathing, let alone whether they're doing it well.

In spiritual terms, the breath is literally the connecting bridge between the soul and the body. This is most obvious, of course, if you've ever seen a corpse: no breath—no life force.

The soul may be alive and well, but it's unable to reside in the body, unless there's the presence of breath to connect the two.

Once you created life with your breath, now comes the question:

"Who are you, who do you want to be, and how do you want to express yourself?" The answer will always be connected to your breath.

Your breath is your first and foremost tool for human self-expression. Most of us, however, don't ever make this conscious realization until much later in our life (like yours truly)—maybe even until today, as you're reading this.

Your voice riding on your breath has certain unique vibrations and frequencies. It can produce different frequencies and effects in different ranges, under different circumstances, with different people, and when experiencing or expressing different feelings.

The easy and effective system you'll discover in the next part of this book will enable you to develop and then choose from the full menu of your voice. The blueprint to your unique, specific menu is already available to you. Once consciously "activated," whether you're a singer or not, you can *always* have full control of how you speak, how you act, and how you feel. Once you have effortless control over your breath and your voice, you can more effectively influence your overall health and happiness.

You need space. So does your body.

Yes, granted, by now you know that strengthening your lungs increases your lung capacity, which strengthens your immune system. But what else is your breath good for, and why am I placing such emphasis on it?

To build your voice—your instrument—from the inside out, you have to start with your breath. That's why the first few tools listed in this book are the ones that develop your breath, in the simplest, most holistic way possible. People are often amazed at how much better they feel even after learning these few, simple practices. So why do you want to develop your breath?

Think of it this way:

Imagine sticking yourself in the middle of the following two things and yelling. Which one would feel more comfortable, and make more sound: a pile of bricks, or a cathedral?

Right. Of course—the cathedral. Why is that?

When you have a large pile of bricks you might have the same amount of physical matter and materials it would take to build a cathedral. But what is different? A cathedral has *space*!

Your body needs *space* to create beautiful, harmonious feelings, vibrations, and sounds.

Using your breath to create more space in your body, as much as you naturally can, allows you to create an acoustic environment similar to that of a cathedral—all in your own body.

Your body is your instrument

If I keep talking about the voice as if it was a physical instrument—that's because it is. When I show you a guitar or cello, and ask you to point to the instrument that makes the actual sound, you would most likely point to the whole thing. Chances are you won't point to just the strings, right?

Buying strings is not enough to create an instrument. You need to hollow the block of wood or metal to create lots of space for the sound to resonate.

And yet so often when you ask people where their voice is located, they point in the general direction of their throat, to indicate the vocal cords only.

Your voice is your whole body.

In order to optimize its sound and make it as effective as it can be, you must first create space in your body—your instrument—and then simply use that open space to set the "strings" vibrating—with your own power.

Bingo.

All these vibrations reach throughout your body, in different ranges, producing different frequencies. All of these vibrations with their respective frequencies are necessary for a holistic voice, healthy body, your overall well-being, and full expression of yourself.

It's when we neglect the totality of our instrument that we start to shrink, contract, feel constricted and suffer, either emotionally, mentally or physically.

So, get ready to build, and open up your cathedral, and let it vibrate with the Divine sounds that are uniquely yours, uniquely healing to your own body, mind, emotions, and your soul.

CHAPTER 8

The Seven Qualities of True Wellness You Must Have to Improve Your Life, Love, Health, and Happiness

Awareness, Relaxation, Alignment, Openness, Flow, Power, Energy.

The trick here is not to simply know about these qualities, or just repeat them as affirmations, but to actually train your body to embody them. Only then will you be able to live according to them.

You see, the body makes something manifest. When it's in the body, you feel it. Imagine, someone caresses your arm. You feel that, right? It feels good. Now imagine that person suddenly pinching your arm. Ouch. You feel it, and it doesn't feel nearly as good.

My point?

Manifest whatever you want in your body first, and you will feel it.

Here we go. Here are the 7 qualities that, if manifested in your body, will make you feel good, resulting in true wellness. Once you really learned this, it'll take you just a few seconds to remind your body!

Here are the 7 Qualities of 7 Seconds to Now

1) Awareness

First, you must be aware. You need to know who you are.

Depending on your nervous system, past karma, desires for your life, you're likely already more or less aware—at least on some level—of who you are."

Take this a step further, and examine awareness in the biggest, most cosmic sense. With this outlook, and maybe even experience, you come to understand that you are One with All, Source, Infinite, Divine.

This knowledge, based on direct experience, is what has been called "enlightenment." Whether you came to this through meditation, some form of yoga, a generally spiritual background, or simply the desire to be healthy and happy, being aware is the first, and most important step of all.

Without awareness, nothing matters. Heck, when we don't sleep enough, our subjective sense of awareness is impaired. When we're awake, our awareness is heightened, and we feel alive. As a result, our health, happiness, well-being, and quality of life improve.

It helps to be rested, for sure, and to incorporate some form of meditation into our life. For me this has been TM, ever since I was 20. After all, life in its purest form *is* pure awareness, so you might as well operate from that level more and more. Also, when we're more aware of each other, on a global level, then we truly have a sense of togetherness, of true community, and of peace on earth.

2) Relaxation

If you're relaxed, everything is easier and more fun. When we're tense it's tough to enjoy anything. There are many ways to become relaxed, and yes, meditation being one of the most profound. But one quick surefire way is to breathe in a way the body responds favorably to. The result? It let's go of any constriction.

There are people around whom we feel so at ease, so comfortable, because they seem to be so easy going and comfortable with themselves. You, too, can train your body to fall into this natural state of relaxation, through meditation, and through correct, simple breathing.

Your whole body functions in a more harmonious way when you feel relaxed, and deeply, profoundly at ease. More ease in your body translates to better health, increased happiness, and more success in life. Rather than getting irritated at one another, we're able to treat each other with ease, understanding, and even humor, stemming from the relaxation we feel in our own body.

Again, for those of you who want to give meditation (TM) a try, here is their website link: tm.org

3) Alignment

Ah, alignment, so wonderful when you've got it, yet so elusive to many. So what exactly is it?

When you're aligned with who you are, who you want to be, and aligned with Source, with Divine guidance, then you are, what many have called, "in the zone." In that special space you feel pretty invincible. No matter what, when you're in your true center, whatever happens, you are: (a) okay, and (b) okay with whatever is.

There are simple ways to get into your center and aligned with the Divine, so you're guided by your Higher Self. Meditation, again, yes, and the physical equivalent—a certain alignment of the body—make you feel really powerful and free at the same time. When each of us is aligned with who we're supposed to be, the whole world will breathe a sigh of relief.

4) Expansion

Have you ever had a great idea, told it to someone, all excited, only to have it shut down immediately? And have you presented an idea to someone who welcomed your idea with an open mind and heart? Which one felt better to you? I know, duh, but hear me out:

Your body doesn't like rejection either; it does not enjoy when you cut yourself off. Your body much prefers when it can flow, roll with the punches, and generally deal with whatever comes its way in a holistic, fluid way.

Dis-ease starts when you're not at ease, when there's resistance—resistance to what is.

Think about it. If there's no resistance to what is, then what, exactly, is there for the body to tighten up about? If it's allowed to flow and be open, there's no chance for it to hold on to anything unwanted. Yes, there is the issue of karma—we just never know which way things will go. But when we can stay open and receptive, we—and our body—have a chance to handle everything with ease.

5) Flow

The logical next step to openness is flow of communication. Many of us have such trouble communicating. Yet if there is flow within ourselves, and our body, then there's a fluid communication between all our chakras, or energy centers. No one part of the body is locked down, no part of the body feels as if it's cut off from the rest. The entire thing functions as one harmonious whole.

On a larger scale, again, too, when there is flow of communication between individuals, families, cities, and countries, there's less chance of friction.

Train your body to allow flow of communication within, and as a result this flow radiates into your environment and beyond.

There are wonderful interpersonal communication techniques out there, btw. to help increase this sort of dynamic. My personal favorite is Marshall Rosenberg's Non-Violent Communication (NVC).

6) Power

You need power if you want to be alive. Life can throw you curve balls, and you better bring your "A-game," right? If you construct in your mind, for a moment, the ideal you—healthy, happy, full of vitality—it's hard to imagine the quality of power missing from the mix. The people we admire in the world have power. Some abuse it, some simply exude it. In any case, your body certainly benefits from strength and power.

Well, how do you get it? Material riches and status used to be what we associated with power, yet you and I know that true power comes from within, from your connection to Source, and to your body.

When you feel powerful you feel invincible, self-sufficient, lovable, strong, and generous. That's a good thing to culture within ourselves, so we can share it with our world, and help others in their moment of weakness. After all, it really is a moment, and nothing more. We all take turns feeling weak, but even in these trying times we must remember our true nature, which is all-powerful, all-Divine.

7) Energy

Ha, there we go. This is my favorite one. Just you wait until you get your hands—or voice—on the exercise later in the book that you use to increase your energy. I'll give you a hint: kids call it the "chattering monkey."

The whole universe is made of energy. Everything we see, hear, touch, and experience is energy. If you've ever seen it, it's a huge, infinite globe of sparkling, lively, infinitely celestial energy, humming, vibrating, from within your own Self.

That's where true energy is: Within. Sure, I love my morning cup of coffee to give me that extra boost, but real energy lives within your body already, since this is all you are.

So get ready for this ride, to make these qualities manifest in your body with the tool you already possess: your voice!

Now that you're primed, let's move on to the actual instructions of Sing Yourself Well.

Enjoy this journey of the discovery of your own unique voice! You might just be amazed.

PART 2

THE HOW TO

The Sing Yourself Well (in 7 Seconds) System

CHAPTER 9

1 AWARENESS

Who? You!

I have a question for you:

- Who is the most important person in the whole world in your life?

- Who is the one that was there at birth, and will be there with you throughout your life until you transition?

- Who is the only person in the whole world you have control over? The only one you can actually change?

Yes, it is you!

—If you replied and pointed to your mom, your boss, your kids, or your grandma, then maybe rewind and do it again. :)

The most important person in your life is **you**. You live in your center. You live from beginning to end, and the more you are aligned with who you are in this life, the happier you'll be.

So right now I want you to actually physically point to that one person who is in charge of your life.

Do it. Point. Yes, exactly.

This is the person who's in charge of your life. Only this person. Not the person over there, not your kids, your spouse, your ever so cute puppy or kitty, not even your boss—not *any* perceived other.

This step is the most important step of all the other steps to follow, because all of those are based on this *one crucial realization*: that **you** are the most important person in **your life**.

We are all One, yes. But when it comes to changing the world, we know by now, it's much harder to affect change on the outside, try as we might, haha.

It's way easier to attend to your own life. Start there, right where you are. Change your frequency, your energy, your feelings, and watch what happens on the "outside." It's quite magical, really.

You know this, of course. After all, you're reading this, eager to learn, grow, change, and get happy!

Point to that person one more time. It's good practice. It'll come in handy later on.

Yes. Good.

This is the gesture you should make second nature. Commit it to your muscle memory. This is and will be **your own personal safety button**.

From now on, any time you feel "off", your immediate response should be: pointing to yourself. You are the center. You are the one feeling good, sad, happy, mad and so on.

Anytime it seems that anything on the outside sets you off, *know* in your bones that it's your own feeling, attitude, and reaction you notice, and **not** the actual event.

People have all kinds of reactions to outside events. Yours is unique to you. Because <u>you</u> are unique. Learn to recognize that right away—every time you notice a reaction in your body other than happy. It'll make your life a whole lot easier!

One more time. Let go of your hand pointing to yourself.

Then ask yourself again:

Who is experiencing this present moment? Who is the most important person, the only one in charge of your life? The only one you have control over, the only one you can change? Go.

Are you pointing to yourself?

Excellent.

This is the key, right here, to becoming **self-referral**. No matter what.

This is the key to taking control of your life.

This is the key to all your creativity.

This is the key to **who you are, why you are here**, and **what you're here to do**.

CHAPTER 10

2 RELAXATION

Rub it Out!

Good.

Now you know who is the most important person in the world—as if you didn't know already, right? :)

Where on your body did you end up pointing?

Most likely your hand touched high up on your sternum, right?

The spot you pointed to is actually a very important point in the whole body:

It's the spot for you to get into your body, to get into your breath, to align with your center. Isn't that interesting?

When you ask little kids: "Where are you, point to yourself, who is the most important person?"

They will most likely say: "Yeah me, me, me, me, I'm the one," or whatever you asked them. And they will most likely point to themselves, to this exact spot.

Very rarely will anyone point to their elbow, their knee or their nose! :)

So, the spot you most likely pointed to, up high on the sternum, is where I want you to touch your fingers to.

To clarify:

Go down about two inches from each of your collar bones, on both sides. Then meet in the middle. It's a point that slightly protrudes high up on your sternum.

This spot is the acupressure point for your diaphragm.

The diaphragm is in charge of your breathing.

It's a muscle that contracts and relaxes, contracts and relaxes.

It allows your lungs to expand, to fill with air and with oxygen for you to live.

When the diaphragm is relaxed you have more room to breathe.

Why?

Because when your diaphragm is relaxed, it drops down into its natural position.

This gives your lungs more space, so they can fill up with more air, and you have more room to breathe!

More air, more freedom, more relaxation and ease!

During the day when we're going about our business—whatever we're doing—we may often forget about our breath.

Whether we're teaching, at work, are a student, or a busy mom—oftentimes we'll get so into what we're doing that we completely lose track of our body.

I know it happens to me, which is why I'm doing this—I'm really creating this course for me. :)

Suddenly we're out of breath, or short of breath, or feel pressure in our throat.

In order to remember to go back to the body you already know the first step:

Oh right: me!

I am the one in charge of my life. I'm the one who can fix myself. Not my kids, or my pets, my husband, or boyfriend, my boss, or my friends.

Yes, all that too, but who is the basis?

You are.

So, you already know who's the basis of your life.

Now you need to give yourself some space, some room to breathe!!

Now you need to enliven *your own* inner center.

And you do that by—ingeniously enough this is how Nature structured it—rubbing this spot, this acupressure spot for your diaphragm.

Rubbing this spot relaxes the diaphragm which can get tight during the day.

Whether we got out of breath jogging, or running around picking up our kids, or we have to give a speech—suddenly we realize we're just breathing really high in our body.

You may have heard someone well-meaning tell you to take a deep breath, to breathe deeply, and so you take a big breath high up, lifting your shoulders.

All of which is the *opposite* of breathing deeply.

This spot right here, this acupressure spot of the diaphragm is in charge of giving you that low breath.

Enlivening this spot gives you that full lung capacity you need to live your life fully and in a relaxed way.

Here's what you do:

Take your fingers—your pointer, middle and ring fingers—and point to yourself high up on your sternum, like you did above.

Simply attach your fingers to your skin there, and with the skin rub the bony part underneath. Rub it really **vigorously**, for about **five to seven seconds** in the beginning.

Later on when you've practiced, it won't take as long. Even 2-3 seconds will be enough.

SING YOURSELF WELL™ IN 7 SECONDS

Important:

Right now it takes this much for your body to understand and learn a totally new way of responding and functioning.

Everything will take a bit longer at first. By the end, the *whole sequence* takes **7 seconds**.

Later on, even just touching there may get you the same results!

But for now you want to get your diaphragm in the new habit of having your help and support in order for your breath to be low and relaxed, so it can keep you healthy.

So, point to yourself, the most important person in the world—you're going to hear me say this a lot—and rub vigorously for about five to seven seconds.

Here's what I want you to observe when you do this—and maybe you can feel it more, when you close your eyes, especially in the beginning:

Watch what happens **inside your body**, in the tummy area.

Maybe you'll feel it right away.

As your diaphragm drops, your tummy pops out, and you may feel the sudden and delightful urge to take a deeper breath.

And because you breathe all the way around—plus your lungs feel like they can breathe more—your sides and your back may pop out a little bit, too. Your lungs have more room to expand now, all around!

Do it one more time.

Rub your acupressure point again, but please not longer than seven seconds. I don't want you to burrow a hole through to the other side. :) Okay, one, two, three, four, five, six, seven.

In the beginning it may help you to look at the video to see if you're doing it right.

But after a while, feel free to close your eyes, and feel into your own body.

After all, that is the whole point: To get into your own self, into your own body.

You may have noticed that your whole body relaxes. Your tummy pops out, and your whole body goes: "Oh thank you. Finally I can breathe again. Finally, there's relaxation. Now I feel cozy in my body."

And the whole goal really, is to feel cozy, comfortable and grounded in your body, and to be fully present in your body. Right?

Do it one more time: point to yourself, and rub that spot for a few seconds. Close your eyes if you want to, and feel how suddenly your tummy pops out and you feel you have more room to breathe, because your lungs can expand.

Great!

Doesn't this feel good? Relaxing? Do you feel the extra ease in your body?

This becomes more and more important as we get older, since with age "normally" our lung capacity may decrease.

Maybe we'll walk a little bit more hunched, or sit around more, or we don't express ourselves, and suddenly we get smaller and smaller, and we shrink.

No! You want to breathe fully! For the rest of your life!

I'm in my late fifties now, and I want to breathe more and more. I want more and more lung capacity. I want to feel taller and taller. I've already grown a whole inch in the last five years. I used to be five ten, now I'm five eleven.

Not that I need to grow anymore. :) But it's nice to feel the expansion.

And the expansion happens from the *inside*.

You can do stretches all day long, pull on this and that as much as you want.

If the lungs cannot support your whole body, then you need to correct that at the base. And the base is you. Your body, your center, your lungs and your diaphragm.

Now you know *how* to do this.

You know how to relax your diaphragm, feel it drop down, feel more air rushing into your lungs, feel your tummy pop out, and feel your whole body relax—maybe for the first time in a long time.

I know it was that way for me.

At some point I was so tight, had so much stress in my life, plus I had a lead role in an opera performance coming up—and I could barely stand straight and take a breath to sing the phrase.

I did Rolfing, and saw a chiropractor, and he had me rub that spot.

Within a few seconds my whole body felt almost reborn. I wanted to cry tears of relief. It was as if the weight of years of tightening up had lifted off of me.

So feel yourself get that extra amount of air. Feel the air and oxygen rush in and your lungs expand. Feel the relaxation in your whole body.

We'll do a little more breath work later on, because it's so basic, so important, especially for non-singers.

For now, just enjoy this feeling of relaxation in your body.

Be aware that every time you point to yourself, you do something good for yourself, your body, and therefore your spirit.

You are the basis for your life. Your whole life experience is right here, in this moment.

And then give yourself that deep, low breath, and you give yourself the lung capacity, the extra health, and the improvement in the functioning of the immune system, all because you're breathing better!

Good.

One last time, rub.

Feel it, feel the relaxation happening in your body. Excellent.

CHAPTER 11

3 ALIGNMENT

Straighten up

Alright, so, to recap:

First step, point to self.

Second step, rub that spot on your sternum vigorously to get your breath low, to get yourself into your body.

Here's the third step.

This is mind-bogglingly simple, and you may have heard it before from your parents or your teachers:

Be straight in your body!

Now, by straight I don't mean rigid like a soldier, chin up high, shoulders squared!

So many of our generation grew up associating straight with that image.

Tell anyone to straighten up, and that's most likely what they resort to.

No!

By straight I mean effortlessly aligned. Like a marionette. With an elongated spine.

Here's the reason why:

When your body is straight, you have more of a chance to be in your center.

Literally. And therefore figuratively.

Test it for yourself in even just these three scenarios:

The next time you don't feel good, are stressed out, or feeling down, I want you to observe what kind of position your body is in:

1) Most likely, if you're worried, sad, anxious, or depressed, you'll be slumped or leaning forward. In any case you'll be hunched, right?

You'll be contracted. Whether you're sitting or standing or even walking.

Pay attention the next time you're in *any other mood* other than happily in your center, okay?

Watch your body in that moment.

When you're afraid of something, observe how your body contracts.

SING YOURSELF WELL™ IN 7 SECONDS

When you're worried about something, notice how you're sitting.

Maybe you'll even have to support your head. Holding your head in your hands is the typical pose when you worry. Right?

Notice, how in all these cases you're leaning forward, contracting your body and your energy.

2) Then, sense your body's feeling and posture, when you're angry:

Maybe the driver in front of you is behaving in a way that just irks the heck out of you. Or your spouse left his dirty socks on the floor, again! Or your mom is lecturing you about how to run your life. Or your kids drive you bonkers.

Watch what your body does:

You may be grabbing the wheel, you'll be contracting against the outside influence, you'll be curving your upper body as if to attack, lash out, or to brace yourself.

Whether you're mad or you're sad, you'll be leaning forward, wanting to protect your heart. You'll be curving and contracting your body and energy.

3) Vice versa, if you're distrustful of someone, you'll be leaning backwards, away from your center in the other direction. Leaning away from the threat to your own inner integrity.

Likewise, if you're afraid of someone, you'll be curving away from the person—backwards to perceived safety and refuge.

In all these scenarios—whether you're leaning forward or backwards—if you and your emotions are *not in your total alignment,* in your happy space, your body will show it!

So, what do you think is the genius, simple way to adjust your emotions?

Just take a wild guess!

Yes!

Be effortlessly straight in your body.

Then watch—and **feel**—what happens with your emotions.

When you look at all the pictures of gurus and saints, watch the position they're in:

Do you see very many who lean backwards, sideways, or bend forward?

No! They are in their center.

Now, they're probably most likely already enlightened, in which case they could be in any other position they wanted to.

But they choose to be in this straight position.

Why?

Because it's the most effortless and healthy position for the body, mind, heart, and spirit.

The body gets happy when it's aligned—and **this is what I mean by aligned**:

Feel aligned upwards from the top of your head to the Heavens.

At the same time, feel aligned downwards from the base of your spine, your tailbone, towards the Earth.

Feel as if a cord of light, a stream of pure light connects you with the center of Earth.

Feel as if that same cord goes up your spine all the way, and connects you with the Heavens far above your head.

Feel this right now. If you want to close your eyes, that's fine. Whether you're sitting or standing right now, either one is fine. Just not if you're driving, please!

Feel as if some **little cherub angels**, or devas, have a light stream attached to the top of your head, and are very gently pulling you up, up, up to the Heavens—very effortlessly, very easily, and blissfully.

Feel as if the same light stream really comes from the center of the Earth, and connects you to it. Imagine there to be a sparkly crystal at the heart of Mother Earth, and from there the light radiates back towards your body.

It happens to align with the tip of your spine, with the base of your spine, and then goes up your spine and into Heaven. Just imagine that now.

This is actually part of what the structure of the Universe is like. Divine Light is at the heart and core of it, everything is "made" of Divine Light, like a huge, infinite crystal palace.

Feel your whole body vibrate on this stream of Light, and get aligned and straight in a very effortless way.

Feel your body straighten effortlessly, **like a marionette**.

You know how marionettes have strings in very strategic places so they're always upright, but they're flexible?

They're not stiff. That wouldn't make a very good marionette—that's more like a scary soldier or a broomstick.

But a floppy, flexible marionette is able to have the head on the neck, neck on shoulders, shoulders on rib cage, rib cage on hips, all in an effortlessly balanced way.

That way, a marionette can "feel" and express every emotion the puppeteer wants it to express, all while staying true to its unique make-up.

Why? Because it's always perfectly aligned with its center.

This is how I want you to feel right now.

See if you can feel that alignment with your center in your whole body right now. Feel this effortless alignment, on your axis, connected to Divine both up to the Heavens and down to Mother Earth.

Feel it, so you can recognize it. That way, whenever you are not in it, you can get back into it, easily, from that *muscle memory* you're establishing now.

Then, the next time you have an emotion that feels like a foreign emotion, an emotion you just don't feel good about—it's not you, you're not happy, you don't feel peaceful, you don't feel blissful, you don't feel at that neutral level of energy—see if you can **feel what your body is doing, and then correct it with your body.**

What's important here is:

Correct it with your body—rather than correcting it from your head, thinking: "Oh I shouldn't be like this. After all, life is bliss. I shouldn't feel this, I shouldn't feel that."

Mental intention is also important, of course—**but the body has to be receptive and able to make it happen.**

Here's an analogy:

It's very, very difficult to plant a beautiful garden, when you're faced with a flower bed that has been officially taken over by weeds.

Now, I happen to love weeds and eat many of them. Weeds are not bad—it's just an analogy.

I planted some basil seeds, sage, rosemary, lavender, and dill in the spring. Also tomatoes, lettuce and mums.

I had to be careful to pluck out all the different weeds first.

Because what happens if I just throw the seeds on weeded terrain? The new plants will get eaten alive by all the weeds. In order to grow beautiful plants, you first need to get the weeds out.

In order to feel happy and plant happy thought and feelings, you want to have your body be in the most fertile position, the most aligned with your own center.

Then you can grow the emotions you do want.

Does that make sense?

In order for you to get the life and body you want—to feel the thoughts and the emotions you want, speak the words you want, take the action you want, *so you can have the experiences you want*—**you have to be in your center**, aligned with your Higher purpose.

Your body will show you how.

For that to happen, you have to help your body!

Align your body with the Heavens, and align it with the Earth.

You are the conduit between the two.

Both are equally necessary in order to live on this Earth.

Aligning your body this way will make it easy for you to come into your center emotionally and with your thoughts.

From there you go forth and do whatever you need to do.

You'll feel freer and clearer, resulting in more evolutionary decision making, and more fulfilling experiences.

This was the third of the most basic seven steps for you to get into your center, and to clear out clutter. From there, your true center of your body, you then create the emotions and the experiences you want to have in your life.

Let's review. Please do it with me:

First, point to yourself. Be **aware**.

Second, rub that spot, to relax and lower your diaphragm. Your lungs expand, you take a deeper breath, and you feel **relaxed**.

Third, effortlessly **align** with your center going up to the Heavens, down to the Earth, in a fluid way.

As you get used to doing this, you may get so good at it, and so attuned, that you'll notice there'll be one point where your body feels particularly nicely aligned.

Sometimes all it takes is moving slightly, either forward or back, straighter or less straight, to feel a shift in how you feel.

Adjusting your body slightly, even just an eighth of an inch, whether you're standing or whether you're sitting, may result in you feeling more or less blissful in your body.

You may try adjusting your pelvis a little bit, you may adjust your ribs a little bit in any kind of direction, until you feel that tingly feeling in your spine. Listen to that tingly sensation at the base of your spine, from where it rises up your spine to your head and beyond.

Weird one:

What I found is that my *actual center is about an eighth behind my middle*. Sounds weird, is true. Try it.

There will be a point when you've played around a little bit, even with tiny little adjustments, where the spine feels so yummy that you think: "Boy, I feel pretty invincible right now. It's really hard to feel miserable right now. Really nice."

Good, so now you know the first three steps in order to find your center.

All with the help of your body! No mindset, thinking, affirmations, or tricking yourself.

Simply attend to your body and the rest will follow.

You don't need to ignore your body, or overcome your body, or dominate your body. Your body will get you there—wherever *that* is, haha!

Your body will get you where you want to be, whether it's running somewhere, or driving, or flying, or going to the restaurant, or sleeping.

Your body will even get you going inward to where you live, to your Self, where your connection is with the absolute, deep inside your own body and mind. Try TM for that profound experience.

Your consciousness envelops the entire universe. With the help of your body you can realize that. You can experience it practically in "I am the Universe."

CHAPTER 12

4 EXPANSION

Dare to Take Up Space!-

This next step, the fourth step, now starts to go in the direction of expanding your voice. With the help of your **breath**, and again with the help of your body.

Because what is your voice?

Your voice is the whole instrument, your whole body. It's not just the voice box.

Just like in a cello or a guitar—there are the strings, which are very useful.

However, if you take the body away from the cello and just have the strings, it's not so useful, right?

Same with your body: **You need your whole body.**

You need the structure, you need the volume, you need the resonance, and you need the space.

You need your body to be big and expanded in order for the air, and for your consciousness to flit around in it—to make beautiful sounds, to make useful sounds, to make pleasing sounds, and to make powerful sounds.

For that you need your body to be in the strongest, most centered, most expanded state.

And what could be a more expanded state than a big yawn?

If you've ever seen a lion or lioness roar or yawn, it's pretty impressive. I mean, if you were really close, it might even border on scary, but for him it feels wonderful. For her it feels wonderful.

That opening into a yawn is one of the most freeing and relaxing states the body can be in, which is why we love to do it. It feels so good that we usually feel we have to cover it up when we're around other people. :)

Try it right now. Yawn to your heart's content.

Go ahead. Yawn. Aaaaahhhhhhh...

If it doesn't come easily right now—although in the privacy of your own home it may be—here's a trick you can use:

Feel as if there's a lift happening inside your mouth, behind where your upper molars end and the little gummy and bony part starts.

Feel as if, again, those little angels or devas are lifting you there.

Maybe there are some very gentle velvet hooks just nudging upwards a little bit. Feel how that is lifting you up high, almost like an inner smile.

Here's the reason why a yawn is so phenomenally relaxing and expansive—in addition to the extra intake of air and oxygen:

There is a coexistence of opposites.

When you yawn, your uvula goes up, and your larynx descends and goes down. Uvula goes up, larynx goes down.

That results in this wonderful, pleasing, pleasurable stretch of a yawn.

Do you feel it? Try it again.

See if you can make yourself yawn. Really feel that lift, up, up, up, up, up, and down, down, down, down, down—that expansion.

You can think of a **Mama lion**. When she roars, or when she yawns, visualize how open her throat is. Maybe she's lying under a tree and she's stretching out with her cubs. This relaxed yawn. You deserve that.

This yawn has a wonderfully relaxing effect on your body.

Here are the reasons why this openness is so very important:

1) Your throat is the center of not just speaking and singing, and general communication, and your voice, but of **self expression**.

When this chakra is blocked, self expression suffers.

The reason we're here together and you're reading this, is, as you know, my own story about this.

One day I heard Deepak Chopra say to me: *You have thyroid cancer. Your chakra of self expression is blocked. If you want to heal, you have to start expressing yourself, speak up and start to sing!*

That was that. It was decided.

At age 32 I started to sing, learn, practice, research, and a few years later, perform, and teach hundreds of women and kids how to sing.

It is vital that we *all* use our full voice. The throat needs that openness so you can feel free, so you can feel heard, so you can express yourself freely!

2) Another reason you need an open throat is to find a **balance between going inward and going outward**.

Find the balance between feeling who you are on the inside—finding your true inner, unique voice—*and* expressing that to the world in all the different ways you're meant to express yourself with your outward voice.

This balance is critically important for a life in equilibrium:

- Find and listen to your inner voice, your dharma, who you are, why you're here, and what you're here to do, give, get, and share.

- Then find your most powerful, authentic outer voice and express it unapologetically in all its glory.

3) The other often forgotten reason why it's so vital to have your throat chakra open—and you can start practicing that with the yawn—is that **the throat is the connection between your heart and mind.**

When this connection is blocked, your *mind* will struggle and feel as if it has to figure out everything by itself.

Your *heart* may want to tell the mind something and can't, because it's like a gridlock, like a traffic jam. You can't get through. Communication is very fragmented, very limited.

You don't want that.

You want to let go of that!

You want to open up so that your mind can speak to your heart, and your heart can get through and communicate with your mind and share its feelings.

Also your gut in your power chakra has a strong opinion about things. You know that, right?

It's not called "**gut feeling**" for nothing. In order for this vital input to get through to your mind, your throat needs to be open!

You need to be heard. You can only be heard if your feelings and thoughts are being expressed, if there's a flow, a frictionless flow to allow for those. That requires an openness in your throat chakra.

The throat chakra is the center of self expression, of communication, and of the voice—of your unique voice.

When this space is expanded, open and free, then the mind will hear the heart, and the heart will hear what the mind has to say, and the whole communication is frictionless.

Divine will be connected with Earth, and Earth will have a channel to voice herself through you and connect with Divine.

So do that one more time.

Yawn to your heart's content.

If you want to make a noise that's fine too. Just yawn. Feel the openness.

What's important here is the **beginning of the yawn**. That is the key point.

In the *beginning of the yawn*—in that impulse to liberate, to open up, to relax—the uvula lifts, and the larynx goes down.

Memorize that. Notice how that feels in your body—that lifted feeling in the *beginning* of your yawn.

If you've ever watched opera singers, they walk around on stage looking as if they're full of themselves, right? And you know what?

They are. They're full of ***themselves.***

They're walking around with that lifted feeling, with that expanded feeling, with that open feeling.

Aligned in their center, connected with Heaven and Earth, their breath is relaxed, and they feel and come across as pretty invincible.

It also looks like they're relaxed, powerful, and yawning or smiling a lot. When you sing with your whole body, this is what you look like. And it feels great in your body.

When your body is not connected with that openness, with that freedom, then it doesn't have the other channels and chakras connected to that.

The beginning of the yawn is the most relaxing point in the yawn.

Everything is wide open and relaxed. For us singers, especially opera singers who need a lot of stamina, resonance, and volume, that expansion lasts throughout all our singing.

Later on in the yawn, once the full expansion has happened, the uvula goes back down, and the larynx comes back up. Everything is more closed again.

So when you memorize what it feels like to feel that expansion—that openness in your throat—memorize the *beginning* of that yawn.

When that first impulse comes to yawn, when you go: "Uh-oh, I'm in public, I'd better cover up," **that** is the feeling you want to memorize, okay?

And hopefully you're reading this in private, so you don't have to feel that constricting energy right now, because, clearly, that would clash with it.

Just feel the freedom right now, feel what it feels like, memorize it.

Memorize the muscle memory. This is important. You want to really, physically, mentally, remember what it feels like to start your yawn, so you can reproduce it at any time.

Recap:

Any time you feel collapsed, you can't express yourself, you feel unfree, you feel shy, or any other unwanted emotion, what do you do?

Whom can you fix?

Yes, **you**!

Give yourself the breath of **relaxation** (you know now how), **align** your body, and then feel that **open** expansion in your throat which is so crucial for your self-expression: Yawn!

It's so vitally important for all the chakras to feel each other, to be in communication with each other—and you start to achieve that through this opening.

So yawn to your heart's content, and I'll see you in the next step.

CHAPTER 13

5 FLOW

Enliven Your Chakras

Good.

First step, point to yourself.

Second, rub, relax your diaphragm. Feel it drop; your lungs expand; you take a deeper breath; you're more relaxed.

Third, align yourself with Heaven and Earth. Feel your center. Be alert to where it feels most yummy.

And fourth, lift behind your upper molars into that expansion, that lift, and that yawn. The two opposites: your uvula going up, your larynx going down. Feel the opening at the *beginning of the yawn*.

Into this opening comes step number five!

You can now place something into this yawn that you've probably been wanting to all along. :)

Sound! Your own sound!

Finally!

Maybe you've done it yourself already, or maybe you've found yourself getting annoyed when someone else did it:

When you're really relaxed and nobody's around, you allow yourself to make a **sound in this open yawn space**, right? Usually high to low. Like a siren. In a very relaxed way.

Have you done it? We breathe up into that yawn, and then aaaahhhh, like a voiced sigh, we slide down, like a siren.

This is a very natural, in-born mechanism, and it's a *life saver*.

It's not just that the throat is open at that point, but you're also using that openness to communicate with your voice.

And in what way are you naturally doing it?

From high to low. From the higher frequencies to the lower frequencies. From the higher chakra to the lower chakras. In one fell swoop. It's genius.

Why are we shutting ourselves up all the time when we want to do that?

Because it's not socially acceptable.

Why is that?

Because people take it to mean that we bore them, that we're not interested in them, that it has something to do with the way we feel about them.

No!

It has everything to do with how *you* feel. How relaxed *you* are, or how in need of relaxation *you* are!

I'm really hoping very soon a society will flourish where this is one of the key things people look for when they judge somebody else to be a **good person**.

When someone is this relaxed, she or he is most likely authentically her- or himself.

Lift in the back of your mouth, open into a yawn, and vocalize high to low, sliding down like a siren. Aaahhhh. Letting out that yummy, voiced sigh, you feel pretty good, right?

Why is that? Because in that moment, with your own voice, with the frequencies of your own voice, *you are healing yourself on the most fundamental sound and vibration level.*

Let me say this again.

When you allow yourself—in the openness and relaxation of your open throat—to use your voice from high to low, from higher frequencies to lower frequencies, from higher chakras to lower chakras, in one fell swoop, you're healing yourself with the **frequencies of your own voice**.

When you use your voice to enliven the upper chakras, the middle chakras, and the lower chakras, you're becoming your own healer.

The frequencies of your own voice enliven the upper chakras, the middle chakras, the lower chakras, your whole energy, and your whole body.

There are people selling healing music and healing sounds and all that, and it's wonderful.

But why not use your own voice, the tool you were born with, a tool you carry around with you all the time anyway?

Why shut ourselves up, in order to listen to someone else, to buy someone else's product, to go to somebody else, just so *those* frequencies can heal you?

When all along you have *your own* instrument and its healing frequencies to heal your own body, to heal yourself.

Therefore: Go into your own body, and use the tool you already have. It's right there.

You just relax it, align it, you expand it, and you open it, and then you simply pluck it, like you would an instrument.

And there you are. Try it.

If with this toned yawn your awareness just feels really buzzy and lively, you know why:

Because you have just created healing sounds everywhere in your body.

With the highest tones you enliven your divine and intuitive chakras.

With the middle tones you enliven your throat chakra, your heart, and your power chakra.

And with the lower tones you enliven the chakras in your lower abdomen, and the base of your spine.

The entire range of human frequencies is enlivened. All the frequencies are enlivened and enlightened with your own voice, with the sounds you produce *in* your own body, *with* your own body.

So remember the next time you feel out of sync, off, and not in your center. You have the tools you need to heal yourself.

One more time:

Yawn. Lift behind your upper molars, opening into a yawn, into the beginning of the yawn when your uvula goes up, your larynx goes down, and you sense that yummy feeling.

Your apple cheeks may even go up a little bit, into a cute smirk or smile. This is good. Keep them lifted this way throughout.

Now inhale gently through your nose. On the exhale, tone from high to low, like a siren—or a waterfall trickling down the mountain.

You can do it on any vowel you want. The vowel "U" pronounced "Ooo" is probably easiest for most, although "Aaah" seems to work great for others. Feel out what is most natural for you, where you feel most open and relaxed.

There you are. You just healed yourself on the level of frequency and vibration—with your own body, with the instrument God gave you. And which, conveniently, you always have with you! :)

CHAPTER 14

6 POWER and EMPOWERMENT

Santa's Ho-Ho-Ho

You now know the first five steps. Good.

The sixth step comes right after you went down like a siren from high to low in the open space of your yawn.

When you're way down low, you'll now use the lower frequencies to enliven your lower chakras. This is where your diaphragm, your tummy muscles, and your whole power center come into play.

What I want you to do next is what I call when I teach kids, "Santa's Ho-ho-ho."

Keep that amused, relaxed look with that lift in the back of your upper molars.

It doesn't drop down, **it stays high and happy**. Watch for those raised apple cheeks of yours. This is important.

Psychology has determined that when depressed people respond to neither drugs nor therapy, and are instead told to simply smile, lifting into a smile in the back of their mouth, they get happy!

Why? Because that physical impulse of a smile sends the message to your brain that everything is fine, and you can think happy thoughts again!

So do this one with me now:

Yawn and make an easy and relaxed sound, from very high to as low as you can go. This enlivens your whole body with the frequencies of your own voice.

Then, when you have arrived at the lower tones, way low in your body, you then use your tummy muscles to pulsate Santa fashion:

You say Ho-ho-ho-ho-ho, all still low in your voice.

Pretend you're Santa just for a minute: **Ho-ho-ho-ho-ho**.

Pretend you're really amused—instead of annoyed or embarrassed that I make you do this, haha.

Now, I know there is something called laughter yoga out there.

I took one lesson years ago and I didn't care for it. I didn't find it very amusing or funny.

I love to laugh, I'm pretty goofy myself, and I certainly enjoy funny movies.

But in terms of its useful effect on the body, I find it more useful to go to the body directly.

Rather than think of laughter, or pretend to laugh, with this here you simply produce the **physical sensation** that is, essentially, laughter.

Because when you do this: Ho-ho-ho-ho-ho, it does sound like laughter, but you are producing the sound straight from your core, straight from your power chakra.

It's not psychological or mental. You do it straight from your body. You do it on a real level, rather than a pretend level.

Because our whole point, after years and decades of spiritual development, is, to get back into our body. It's time to integrate all experiences into our body.

This is why you're here, right? To make your spiritual experience manifest. To align with who you are, feel who you are on the inside, and express that powerfully on the outside. For a healthy body, mind, heart, and spirit.

So you want to get into your body, and you do that by expanding, aligning, putting your own frequencies there, and then simply using your tummy to produce these shaking pulsations. Ho-ho-ho-ho-ho.

Okay so just say it with me now: Ho-ho-ho-ho-ho., in a really exaggerated way. Good.

Keep that inner smile, keep that feeling of the lift at all times, even when you are down low in your voice.

It's almost as if you are saying Hee-hee-hee-hee-hee in the back of your mouth, while saying Ho-ho-ho-ho-ho in front.

Think of a **cartoon character**, okay? Hee-hee-hee, like the joker. Keep the lift behind your upper molars.

In the yawn it's easy to keep that lift, it comes naturally. This is how God designed it.

But even when you're done with the yawn, feel as if you are still smiling upward, as if the lift continues. Even when you go down with your voice.

This coexistence of the two opposites is important. This is what opera singers do for hours!

Keep the lift in the back, and then simply add Ho-ho-ho-ho-ho from your power chakra, from your diaphragm, from that pulsation.

You can try it on H, as in Ho-ho-ho at first, and later on just on O, Oh-oh-oh-oh-oh.

Your throat is just open and relaxed, and all the work is done in your power chakra, by your tummy muscles and diaphragm. Oh-oh-oh-oh-oh, on the same breath.

There's a reason why you want to enliven your power chakra. Can you guess?

Yes!!

It's the seat of your own personal power!

We tend to give our power away.

We're forever looking for other people and to other people.

Whom can we help, how can we help, this person wants this, this person needs that, let me just do this for you, and oh, I guess I have to do it this way, and yes, of course I'll do it this way.

And so on, and so on.

Believe me, I know.

I grew up in Germany with a lot of authority around me, and it was really, really hard to find my own center as a child and teen.

That really only happened once I found **TM**, and started to meditate, and found my own inner center that way.

Then once more, when I moved to America, went through my health crisis, and **Deepak Chopra** said: *Okay, wake up, you need to express yourself! You're not just transcendence, you're not just there for other people. You have to get into your own center, and learn to use your voice.*

From then on I've been paying more and more attention that I stay in my center—and if I'm not in it, then I know how to hop right back into it, through these simple, yet profound physical and vocal steps!

It took me seventeen years to figure it all out and to put it together into this system, which you now have.

Seriously, if I had had these steps back then, it would have saved me years of my life! But everything happens for a reason, and in its own good time.

Here you are now, reading what I've learned, and I'm so happy to share it with you!

All, so you can now create your own life in a more enlightened, healthy, and fulfilled way, and so you can share yourself and your message easier, and with many more people.

So, go into your body, into your own center, and use your body to heal yourself.

Be aware of your power center for a moment.

Are you giving away your control to other people? Feeling like a victim, always thinking others are in charge of your life?

Or are you holding on tightly there, because you don't want to give away control?

Neither of those extremes are ideal, or healthy for you in the long run.

I know people who are really tight, insecure, and afraid, and are therefore controlling and manipulative of others.

Because that's what it is, isn't it?

When someone's afraid, they get tight and feel they need to control others, their circumstances, maybe even control themselves, because **they're too afraid to let something greater than themselves take over**.

I'm not talking about not putting your attention on what you want and taking steps to get there. Of course that's what you want to do.

After all, whatever you put our attention on, grows stronger in your life. So go for it, yes. In the Highest Good for all, always!

And **then let it go!**

This is why you're here.

You want that something greater, which is your Highest Self, God, Divine, Creation, Source, Mother Nature, to be in charge fully.

Because only then can you truly be who you are—who this precious jewel is that you're here to be and to sparkle.

You want to align yourself with that Higher power.

You don't want to be small anymore, you don't want to contract. You don't want to be scared. You don't want to just do for others.

You want to be in your center fully, because when you're in your center, aligned with who you are in this life, then you serve creation the best. The fullest. Then you can truly give.

And for that, this tiny little, simple exercise of strengthening your diaphragm, strengthening your power chakra with these pulsations will help you get there!

It seems so simple doesn't it?

It seems crazy simple that these tiny little steps, aligning with your body—how your body is supposed to work anyway—would bring you into your center, into your power, into your expansion, into your alignment, into your freedom of flow, of expression, and of communication.

It's so amazingly simple.

One more time, from the beginning:

Point to the one person who's in charge of you, who can change your life.

Yes, **you**, good.

Relax your breath, rub that acupressure point for the diaphragm, to give your lungs the room to breathe they deserve.

Good. Did you feel it?

It's amazing. Do this whenever you have to give a speech, or you record a video, or you're going in front of your class, your kids, your partner, or your clients. Even before going to an appointment, out to shop, or a walk, if you have some anxiety, or feel flustered. Sit in your car for a minute and just do this and get yourself into your body.

It's a miracle.

Then, **align**, be straight.

Open into a yawn. Enjoy the freedom of that yummy feeling you create with your own body. Simply by opening your throat and letting all the chakras communicate.

Then you put the frequencies of your own voice into that opening, to **enliven** all your chakras, and create **flow**. Singing, or toning highest part of your voice, to lowest part of your voice, like a siren.

Once you're at the lowest part of your voice—keeping the lift of the yawn, smiling in the back, as in Hee-hee-hee—you add Santa's Ho-ho-ho-ho-ho. The pulsation, your **power**, comes from your power chakra.

And when you engage these tummy muscles, a miracle happens:

Your throat will relax even further!

Your throat will realize: "Hey, it's safe for me to be open, because somebody else is in charge. The tummy muscles in the power chakra are supporting me, so **it's safe to be open. Yay!**"

The One who is actually in charge is Divine, Nature, God, cosmic power.

Divine gets expressed through your body, through using the cosmic power your physical body has. Physically, most obviously, it gets expressed through your belly, your power chakra.

Can you feel that, yes? When you do it right, you may feel like a martial artist, always ready, feeling powerful, and almost invincible.

This pulsation of Ho-ho-ho, this being in your body and allowing your power chakra to function normally the way it's designed, will make your throat feel like: "Oh good, finally, I can open up, I can relax. It's safe. I don't have to push, I don't have to press."

If you're a **singer,** at this point you'll be nodding, because you know you cannot possibly make free sounds, full sounds, when your diaphragm is tight, and collapsed, when your lungs can't expand, and when your tummy muscles don't support.

You need that support.

Here's an analogy I use to describe the way your power center upholds the freedom of your throat center:

Have you ever been to a department store where they had one of those fans, on top of which they float a beach ball?

The beach ball and the fan are not touching.

If they were touching there would be shredded plastic everywhere, right?

The fan is the motor that keeps the ball afloat.

Your diaphragm and your tummy muscles in your power chakra are the motor, and your voice box and vocal cords in your throat chakra of self expression are the beach ball.

When your power chakra is engaged and works, then your throat can be open, your voice can be free. Your vocal cords will be vibrating freely, without any strain.

Your voice will have natural power, you'll be able to speak and express yourself with your full authenticity and confidence.

One more time: Yawn. Keep that inner smile.

Then, on your exhale, slide down the scale from high to low.

Once you've arrived on the lower notes, pulsate your tummy muscles as in Ho-ho-ho-ho-ho. Bingo.

Congratulations. You just empowered yourself! Physically.

CHAPTER 15

7 ENERGY

Chattering Monkeys

Now you know

1) **who** you are, you know where you live,

2) how to **relax** your breath and yourself,

3) how to **align** and be straight,

4) how to expand and **open**,

5) how to use that expansion to let **communication** between your various chakras **flow** by sounding the frequencies of your own voice into that space and enliven all your chakras, and

6) how to easily and effortlessly strengthen **your power** chakra, so you are in fact in charge of your life, saying Ho-ho-ho-ho-ho low in your voice.

Now, in this next step, the last and seventh step, you use the same pulsation to send all the frequencies of your voice everywhere in your body.

This creates a burst of energy in the respective chakras and in between, throughout your whole body.

This is how it goes:

You siren down, and you use your Santa Ho-ho-ho-ho-ho, with the pulsation of your tummy muscles, like before.

Now, this time, instead of staying low in your voice, you send your voice up and down your whole body, with the same pulsations.

Yes. Like a monkey. :)

Start low, go higher and higher up with your voice, and then come back down. First do it on Ho-ho-ho. Then gradually switch to Hu-ho-ha-he-hi on the way up. And Hi-he-ha-ho-hu on the way down.

Please note: For simplicity's sake I'm listing the European/Sanskrit pronunciation. The English pronunciation is Hoo-ho-hah-hay-hee on the way up. And Hee-hay-hah-ho-hoo on the way down.

It sounds silly doesn't it?

Which is why when I teach kids, I call it chattering monkeys.

You know why. Tummy area: Ho-ho-ho-ho-ho.

Then up: Hu-ho-ha-he-hi.

And down: Hi-he-ha-ho-hu.

Side Note: I will go into this in another book, but the different vowels actually represent the energies of the different chakras.

Your throat is open, the space behind your upper molars is lifted. You feel the same beginning of the yawn, the same expansion.

Feel the same freedom in your throat as when sliding down with your voice, as if you're feeling really important, all puffed up, and you just have to say something really important, like for example, Ho-ho-ho-ho-ho. And then you go up and down: Up: Hu-ho-ha-he-hi. Down: Hi-he-ha-ho-hu. Very expanded and exaggerated.

You want to exaggerate, because with exaggeration the body will get that freedom, that playfulness.

So feel really expanded, slide down and pretend you're Santa. With this you enliven your power chakra and feel that all your power comes from there, whether you're speaking, thinking, feeling, acting. All your power comes from there.

It allows the throat chakra to be open and relaxed so that communication is good.

Then, when you have enlivened your power chakra, and the lower chakras with your low notes, then from that basis, from that springboard, you can use your voice to send your frequencies and vibrations of all the other notes on your scale up throughout your body.

Practice sending your voice up and down, however high and low you can go.

Just make sure it is on top of the springboard that is your diaphragm, supported by your tummy muscles.

You may find over time not only does your lung capacity increase, but your vocal range may also increase.

You'll be able to use all those wonderful emotions in your communication, within your own body, and with your surroundings.

You'll feel clearer, more confident, more authentically you.

Your message will be heard more clearly, with more authenticity, clarity, confidence, and power—whether you communicate your message to your children, to your clients, to your partner, or to the whole world.

Why?

Because you've enlivened all the chakras in your body.

You've **relaxed** your breath, therefore you.

You're **aligned**.

Your throat chakra is **open**, and now allows free **flow** of communication between all your different chakras, keeping you healthier.

Your **power** chakra is strengthened, so vital for you to feel strong inside of yourself, without feeling controlling.

And now you finally add the playful, sparkly **energy** of enlivening all the chakras with your own voice, so you can use different tones in your voice when you speak.

You can use the higher voices, the lower voices, the very high voices and the very low voices. Not just in terms of the sound, but also expressing the quality of your emotions.

The heart for example, is in the middle chakra.

Many of us talk mainly in that middle range of throat, heart and sometimes power chakras.

With these tools, instead of just talking in that range with those twenty percent of your voice, you're now enlivening all your other tones, frequencies and emotional vocabulary as well

That allows you to make use of all the upper higher chakra frequencies guiding your intuition, your mental clarity, and your decisive intellect—and the lower chakra frequencies with your earthiness, your sensuality, and your creativity. Plus your power chakra, your heart, and self expression.

Everything now gets included and expressed.

So one more time, take that yawning breath, and siren high to low, then pulsate Santa's Ho-ho-ho, enlivening your power chakra from here. And now finally playfully send up your voice all the way throughout your body. Hu-ho-ha-he-hi. Hi-he-ha-ho-hu. Up and down, up and down.

You can probably feel how it's shaking your tummy.

That's good, that's wonderful.

It shakes out all the stuff you don't want and need anymore, all the tightness, all the unnecessary control, and all the insecurity, shyness and loosy-goosiness.

It shakes it all out and instead puts into your body what is truly your strength, where your innate power truly is.

With this your throat chakra can relax and open, and you can send your own healing sounds as energy bursts throughout your whole body to enliven everything in your existence. Good deal?

This will create a new vocabulary for you to draw on.

You had all those emotions tucked away, but they had nowhere to go before.

Now you've created a pathway that is super fluid, where all the emotions are being heard simultaneously and can be expressed at your discretion.

Any time you say anything, or you give a speech, you need to speak from your heart, of course. But you also need to speak from your gut, from your earthiness, from your creativity. You need to speak from your clarity of intellect, from your intuitive powers, your Divine guidance.

All of that will now be more connected and holistically expressed through you. You'll communicate and express yourself through your body, through the Divine channel you are in this life.

Here you go, one last time with my guidance, before I let you lose to practice on your own.

By now you may be so good at it already, it may be so automatic that it takes you much less time than it did in the beginning, right? You'll know you've perfected it, when you can do the whole sequence in 7 seconds.

1) **Who** is the most important person, the one who is in charge of your life, the one who'll make the biggest difference you can possibly make in your life, and in the life of everyone on Earth?

You, yes!

2) Now rub that spot on your sternum to **relax** your diaphragm, and feel it drop and feel your lungs expand.

You have more room to breathe. Good, feel that expansive feeling in your torso.

3) Your body is naturally **aligned**, feeling tall, reaching up to the Heavens from the top of your head, and down to the Earth from your

tail bone, aligned with both in a super fluid way. Find that yummy spot, where you feel blissful in that alignment.

Remember, be straight in your body and your emotions will align with that physical centeredness.

4) Then yawn, feeling a lift behind the upper molars, up, up, up, and down, down, down, enjoying that **open**, relaxed expansion.

5) Place your voice into that space you created, high to low—into the open space that creates this beautiful **flow** of connection between heart and mind.

Feel how this makes you feel sparkly and clear in your head, because finally everything is aligned, open, and communication within your body is flowing freely.

6) Next, use your **power** chakra low in your voice, Ho-ho-ho-ho-ho, Santa style, so you're fully engaged in your power center.

7) Lastly, enliven all the chakras with the **energy** of your voice going up the scale and down again, throughout your whole internal body: Hu-ho-ha-he-hi. Hi-he-ha-ho-hu.

Very important again is this point:

Don't make any sound unless your tummy muscles are engaged, and all your power comes from here.

The throat is simply open and you make high and low sounds, which change with the length of your vocal cords. This makes the notes sound different, but there's no effort involved up in your throat.

The tongue is loose, the jaw is loose, the throat is opened, and all this is possible because your power center works overtime.

But it is meant to work overtime.

So go to your power, go to your core, and with that pulsation send those sparkly energetic frequencies throughout your body!

Enliven your whole body with your voice.

All your communication will be better and easier within your body, resulting in better health, and more happiness inside yourself, and outside with your environment—because you're finally in touch with the whole huge range of vocabulary you have been given. It just was buried until now.

I hope this is fun for you, and a whole new world opens up for you in every moment.

A world of awareness, relaxation, alignment, clarity, ease, openness, confidence, better communication, empowerment, energy, your own inner Divine guidance, and your own inherent power. All it takes is 7 seconds.

And Finally: Conclusion and Send Off!

So this is what the 7 Second **Sing Yourself Well** System does for you. Yes, of course it increases your lung capacity, and strengthens your immune system, releases endorphins and makes you happy. But clearly, as you now realize, the magic lies in more than that. This 7 second system

- Centers you in yourself.

- Helps you relax your breath in the most natural way.

- Aligns you with Heaven and Earth.

- Opens your body to health and flow.

- Enlivens frictionless communication between the different parts, the energy centers or Chakras, of your body.

- Establishes you in your own power.

- Energizes your body and spirit in a fun, efficient and profound way.

There is no way your brain can maintain an emotional downward spiral, when you apply these seven, very **physical tools**.

Within seven seconds your body will be reset by you to come back to at least a neutral position. With your own breath and voice.

Usually my clients, students, and kids I teach in schools tell me that at the end of those seven steps they are bouncing up and down, they're laughing, they're *joyful*, they have their energy back up—and they can't wait to continue with life before it got all dark and weird!

So learn those tools, practice them, and use them.

You then have a means—any time something wants to pull you below the surface—to get back up really fast.

And that is the key, that is the beginning of clear thinking, clear feeling, being in your center, and being in your power.

Then you can make better choices, choices for more energy, for better health, for better habits, for being around the right people, for taking the right action steps in your business, for all these many expressions of yourself, for all your creativity.

But you have to come to that neutral point, and have the tools to come at least to that—as fast as possible.

I'd be hard pressed to tell you if there's anything I've found that is faster than the 7 Seconds **Sing Yourself Well** System.

I clearly have not come across it because otherwise I'd be peddling that! :)

But this is something I've developed in my seventeen years of research, of teaching, of self-exploration, of performing, of having clients, and of teaching students.

SING YOURSELF WELL™ IN 7 SECONDS

Those seven steps are unbelievably powerful, and I cannot wait to hear from you what your experience is, how many times you use them, and how it's helping you.

If now, this all has whetted your appetite for more energetic healing work, I invite you to stay on for the bonuses, to learn additional healing tools to get you into a better place, fast. After all energy is what we, and everything are made of. Clear yourself energetically, and then set your own frequencies vibrating within your body.

As you realize now, singing has benefits way beyond increasing your lung capacity, strengthening your immune system and making you happy.

It profoundly changes the way your body-mind-spirit connection functions, which in turn has profound benefits for how you feel in any given moment And as we know, we only ever really have this moment. If we make the best out of it, the future takes care of itself.

So start today. Start in this moment. If you don't like this moment, use the 7 steps and take charge of the moment from that more neutral place.

Who knows, maybe you're now on your way to a whole new you. Maybe your appetite is whetted, and you can't wait to sing more, play more, and attune your body to the grand cosmic symphony, all because you woke it up to its own, inner energy, frequency, and power.

That's what had happened to me.

In that case, congratulations! Find an aria, an uplifting song, ideally sung by someone with really good "technique," meaning they don't hurt their voice, ever, and instead make full use of their voice's full potential. Find that song, listen to it, feel it, sing it, and make it part of how your body creates, of how you want to feel more, and be more.

There is, of course, much more, and we barely scratched the surface in this book. If you'd like to know more, or find out about any upcoming book, or video training, feel free to register and get onto the VIP list at SingYourselfWell.com.

And if now you're really discovering your own voice and want more training, feel free to contact me. I'll also let you know when my **Ultimate Singer's Guide** as well as **Soprano Master Class** are coming out. Again, just get onto the VIP list at SingYourselfWell.com.

I'll see you soon, and in the meantime: Sing Yourself Well!

Love and Light always,

~ Ulrike

~ This is the official End of the book ~

However, for those of you who enjoy subtle energy healing tools, here are 3 Bonuses. These will help speed up your healing, give you strength, make you feel loved, and train you to use your intuition, all of which will enhance your wellbeing, health and happiness. :)

If subtle energetic healing tools are not your thing, you may skip this section. Thank you for taking this journey with me.

Enjoy and Sing Yourself Well! <3

PART 3

YOUR HEALING BONUSES

BONUS #1

SELF LOVE

It's All in Your Hands

Here is something love-y. :)

Profound, simple, effective, fast. Yet ever so love-y!

Ready?

It took me a while to figure it out, but at some time during giving hundreds of healing voice sessions there was a point where this just simply popped up. And it's genius:

Do you have moments when you'd love to be held, snuggled and loved?

Or even if that's not what you need, you'd love to feel loveable, and feel that in a physical way?

You just crave it, and if there's nobody around to give it to you, you feel sad, your energy is low, and maybe that's why you don't get as much done, and you just feel off.

Of course you now know how to not feel off, right?

You simply follow the tools you already learned, those seven steps that will get you into your center, clear out any gunk, and get you so aligned that you just cannot help but bubble with the joy that is already in you.

Yes? Good!

Now, if there's that day or minute, where you wish there was someone giving you the love you know you deserve, that loving hug—here is a **sweet tool** you can use when you have nobody to hug you and love you physically:

Take your hands—luckily you already have your hands with you—and rub them together for a second or two, to give yourself some energy.

Put some energy into your hands, and cross your hands over at your wrists.

Then place your hands onto your face, crossed over. Now, just rest your face in your hands and relax. Feel your hands caressing your face. It feels really good, right?

SING YOURSELF WELL™ IN 7 SECONDS

The key here is to be inward enough so you can feel your hands caressing your face. You can try closing your eyes.

It's as if somebody else is touching your face, and you simply place your palms onto your face where it feels good.

Try placing your hands on your forehead, your temples, your cheekbones, your chin, and your jaw bone, maybe your nose and mouth, too, but especially those places all around your face.

For some reason your cheekbones may feel particularly good.

Let's try it and then I'll explain to you why this works so well.

Rub your hands together a little bit, cross over your wrists, and then simply place your palms on your face.

You may feel that the energy is mostly in your palms.

It radiates into your fingers too, but mostly you want to use your full palm, full contact on your face.

Wherever it feels good to you, just leave your hands there for a few seconds, then move them to another place that feels good.

Here we go:

Rub together, cross over, put your hands on your face, as if somebody else is caressing it. Forehead, and temples, and cheek bones.

If you want to be particularly brave, and no one is within ear shot, you could even say out loud: "Oh, you're so cute, you're so loveable, oh, I love you so much."

Just rest in that embrace for a few seconds.

How does that feel?

The magic is in the crossed-over hands.

You know why?

Well, what happens if you place your hands on the same side of your face? Ring any bell? Hands to face, right hand on right side, left hand on left side:

Nooooo!!! We do this when we're worried, when we're scared, when we're freaked out by something, when we're saying or thinking: "Oh my God, oh no, oh dear." Right?

We don't want that. We don't want self-hands. We don't want the same hands on the same sides of our face.

For two reasons, the *crossing-over of your hands* is so key:

1) First of all, of course, it feels like somebody else is touching your face, caressing your face. Somebody else is telling you how loveable you are.

Maybe you were lucky enough as a child when someone came and cupped your face in their hands, and it felt so good, and they would maybe even pinch your cheeks—which was somewhat less enjoyable. :)

But they came from their side putting their right hand on your left side, and their left hand on your right side.

This tool mimics the love that comes from somebody else. Your body knows which hand it is simply by the way it feels.

Do it right now. Can you feel the difference? Between same side hands and opposite side hands?

See if you can feel it in your whole body, especially in your tummy area.

2) The second cool reason why this works so well, is this:

The right side of your body represents your masculine side.

The left side of your body represents your feminine side, your female side.

When you cross over your hands, you give **your own masculine energy to your female side,** reassuring you that you are indeed loveable, filling you up with that masculine energy, on your female side.

Conversely, your left hand touches the right side of your face, giving **your own feminine energy to your masculine side**, making you feel loveable. For example, if you're working really hard, this will make you feel cozy and taken care of.

Both happening at the same time creates a feeling, a vibration in your body that feels like **joy**, reassurance, **love** and coziness.

Let's try it again.

Rub your hands together just to get them warm and get some energy flowing.

Cross hands over at your wrists, and place your palms on your forehead, temples, cheekbones, and jaw.

Feel your face relax into your hands, and feel your hands touching your face. It's both at the same time.

There is a **union** happening, an integration happening that is super, super powerful.

Do you feel it?

Do you feel the difference between placing same side hands onto your face, and doing it the correct way, each hand touching the opposite side of your face? Giving yourself that extra bit of energy?

Good.

The next time you don't feel loved, remember you have your own love inside all the time.

SING YOURSELF WELL™ IN 7 SECONDS

Simply apply it: place your opposite hands onto your face, and feel it.

Allow yourself to feel the point of contact on your face. It's called my self-love exercise. You give love to yourself with your own tools.

You have all the tools, right? Just use them. You didn't know. Now you do.

When you do it right, there's a feeling inside your body that feels so cozy that you may finally be able to let go of any wounds, pain, sadness, anger, or grief which you didn't want to acknowledge before.

For so long you may have pushed it down because you need to accomplish, be tough, and show a strong woman or man to the world.

It's possible that the little child wakes up, and you just start sobbing.

It happened to me, and it happens to many others.

It happened to someone who had suffered a stroke.

When she was recovering from the stroke, I taught her this, and she just sobbed for several minutes. She allowed herself to feel all that love welling up inside her, and it washed away all the pain.

She's been fine ever since.

So, enjoy that feeling. Really surrender to that embrace you're giving yourself.

Don't worry if something bubbles up in the body. It's all connected.

If you give yourself love, it's very possible that everything is relaxing and expanding, and you're feeling so loveable.

Then when the relaxation and the expansion happen, it's possible there is some release in the body.

Maybe you start feeling something very deeply, or you may start to cry. Stay with that emotion. Stay there, allow it, and keep loving yourself.

Be present, be there for yourself, give yourself that love, and feel your love. It all is love anyway. Just dissolve whatever is not presenting itself as love, into love. Whatever it is that wants to bubble up.

Don't be scared of what is in there.

It has to come out anyway—it might as well come out through love.

Bring in the light, dissolve the darkness. Bring in the love, dissolve anything that is not love.

It's all in your hands!

Stay tuned for **Open Your Voice to Love.** How to Love yourself fully, so your Love opens to you.

BONUS #2

INTUITION 101

Your Body Knows Your Truth

Here's another tip for you. This one's called Intuition 101. I had posted my first Intuition 101 video on youtube in the spring of 2012.

Why did I call it that?

It's such a basic tool, and you already have it in your body, all ready to use.

I called it 101, because there's nothing more basic than this.

Yet it hasn't been taught, it hasn't been around, it hasn't been something you grew up with, something your parents taught you, or your grandparents, or your school, or your teachers. Nobody teaches this.

So, if you have children, teach them this tool. It'll make their life so much easier.

It'll get them self-referral.

It'll get them finding out: Is this really something I want? And that feels good to me?

Or is this something my peers want for me, or that stranger wants from or for me?

Is it actually something that feels right in my body?

Or is it something that just doesn't feel good in my body at all?

For now I will teach it to you, and if it works for you, please teach it to your children.

You've probably been in a situation when you had the choice between two things, and you just didn't know which one to choose.

You were going around in your head, evaluating all the pros and cons, this and that, is this good, or not good, and you just couldn't figure out what to do.

So what did you do? You went and asked all your friends: "Well, what do you think? Should I do this, or should I do that, because I sure don't know."

Your friends were happy to give you their opinion because you asked them.

And what did you do with their input?

You did exactly the opposite, right?

You've been there, right? I have, for sure.

I'm really happy to be able to tell you a secret:

You are the friend you can ask next time.

You're the one to turn to. You're the one to make your decision for you.

Your intuition is part of your body, part of your consciousness your body lives in, and part of the consciousness that lives in your body.

Use it. Use it as a tool.

This is how it works:

Next time you want to find out whether to do A or B, purple or yellow, up or down, cold or warm, whatever it is, whenever you have two or more options...

When you don't know which one to use: Ask your body. Then listen for the answer.

Give your body the first option and watch what happens.

You can start with something really small. Something you already know the answer to. That makes it easier to get attuned to your body's response.

Start with your name. You know your name. Think your name, feel your name, say your name, sing your name, and just be with your name.

While you do this, watch what happens in your body.

"Yes!":

Most likely your body will feel relaxed, warmer, lighter, and more open, as if all your chakras are opening all over the place. That is a "Yes!"

Your whole body will have a forward motion, as if it wants to take off.

It's literally as if everything in your body is open and warm and wants to go with it. Literally, going with it, **going forward** with what you have just said. In this case it was your name.

Now think of a different name.

Think of your pet's name, Fido or Rover, or somebody else's name. Opposite gender works really well. Something that is definitely not your name.

As much love as you may have for that person or being, it is not your name.

Think of that strange name and watch what happens to your body.

See if you can feel it.

"No!":

Your body may **go backwards** instead of forwards. It closes down, and recedes a little bit. Everything closes, and it gets colder, and heavier. It may be very subtle, or it may be that your body leans back so much that you bonk into your wall.

Do you feel that?

When something is not true for you, without any value judgment in general or how it applies to other people, your body will tell you.

The body will as if say: "Yeah, I don't think so. Last time I checked that wasn't my name." It'll be closing down, going backward, getting cold and heavy.

Maybe if it's a scary thing you're thinking of, i.e. whether to do a certain activity, then you might get a tummy ache. There may even be some wooziness or a cold feeling, maybe you even start to sweat—in any case everything contracts and retreats.

Watch for that reaction.

It means, **right now in the moment you're asking the question**, it's not a good choice for you.

Maybe down the line somebody says: "You know, you should really jump off that cliff, it's really good for you, especially if you're scared."

At that point, again, check in with yourself.

If you feel: "Yes, you know what, this feels pretty good, feels pretty light, feels pretty forward moving. I think I'm going to do it," then that's different.

But in the moment that it's presenting to you, be alert.

Do the seven steps first. Get into your center first.

This is important!

Create full communication between all your chakras first, so that your intuition really works, and you don't get mixed messages: The heart wants one thing, the mind wants another thing, the lower chakras want another thing, your Divine chakra feels another thing.

No. It has to be all aligned—that's the whole purpose of this training, right?

So align yourself, and then sit with your options.

Everything in life is an option. Everything is either yes or no, hot or cold, left or right, up or down. Every single decision is either a yes or a no. Little ones, tiny ones:

"Should I eat white bread or sprouted whole grain bread?" I don't know, ask your body.

There is no one right decision for everybody in the whole world.

You make your decision for you, only you. Another person makes it for them, I make mine for me—for each physiology there will be a different decisions.

We all have to become self-referral, meaning we open and align and expand our own consciousness, our own being, our own body, and work with the tools we've been given.

Not somebody else. Not someone in the media and on television. As in, if you buy this gadget, or this toy, or this car, it's the latest, and it'll help you be happy. No! Use your own tools.

You have them already. If you didn't know you had them so far, that's okay. **You do now.**

So do your seven steps. As we know, the more you practice, the quicker they go, and it can be 7 seconds or less and you're in your center.

Okay, do them right now, with me:

One, two, three, four, five, six, seven.

Okay. Great. Done. Do you feel that sparkly, yet grounded, energized clarity and power? Yes? Now:

Ask your question.

If you actually have a question now, ask your body inwardly. If not, wait, close your eyes, tune in and think of something you really have a question about.

Whatever decision you have to make, watch what your body does.

Your body will tell you the answer.

If it feels warm, if it feels light, open, and there's a forward feeling—it feels as if your body just wants to take off—it is a **YES**.

If there's openness all over the place, in all your chakras, that means it's a YES for you, meaning, it's a good thing for you in the moment you're asking.

And of course everything is in the moment. Whenever you want to find out something, it's in that moment you ask.

Not for the future, not for the past, not for someone else.

We all live in our past and future too much.

If you can ask right now, this is all you need to do, this is all you need to know, and then you go about your business.

You keep aligned with Divine and with Earth moving as you, only as you, and as that you ask the question: "Is it good for me? Bad for me?"

Not some external anything. It's in you. The intelligence is in your body.

If you have something right now, think about it. You can even ask about a specific situation. Do I like this situation? Is this situation in my highest good? Is it in my highest good to eat this food? Is this activity, this person, good for me?

Whatever the question is—always say: "Is it in my **Highest Good**, and in the highest good for everyone?" Your body will know.

So feel it out now. Is your body saying: "Oh yeah baby," all over the place? Everything opening up, leaning forward, leaning into it, moving with it, getting warm and light like you want to take off?

Or is it feeling... hmm... I'm not sure?

Is it telling you maybe not now? Everything closes and the body moves backwards? Maybe your body feels cold and heavy, and it's just not the right thing right now? Or even a most certain **No!**?

You go with what's the right thing for now, until you have another question. And then you can ask again using this tool.

Over time it'll become automatic.

It's not even going to be a big deal anymore.

You'll get so attuned to your own inner alignment that it's like magic. You just want to know something, ah, and you feel it, you got it.

I've been doing this for a long time now. I've been meditating for thirty seven years, and I've been doing my intuitive work and healing voice yoga for seventeen years.

I can feel on a very, very subtle level if something is good or not good. For myself and oftentimes for others, too. Even foods, I can smell them just thinking about them.

Somebody tells me about someone somewhere else, anywhere in the world really, even if I don't know the person, and I can pick up on it. I don't know why, but it's just a skill I have. It's like tuning into a TV channel. Like going to the library and picking out a certain book and reading it.

The one moment where it became very clear to me that my intuition was starting to work amazingly well was when my ex-husband, I and my young son, one and a half years old, were on a beach on the East coast.

It was a pebble beach that went on for miles and miles, a little bit of sand, mostly pebbles. It was beautiful. Nobody was around, it was windy and cool, and we were all bundled up.

We locked the car, and whoever was driving at the moment took the keys. No mention of names.

We walked and walked and walked.

It was so beautiful, the waves were rolling in, the salty sea and beach air smelled so good, and the wind was in our hair. We were just so happy.

Until... we realized we wanted to go back to the car, and for some reason the keys were not—with us—anymore....

We were out in the middle of freaking nowhere with no car keys.

We didn't know where they could be, because we thought we had them on us.

The person who was driving was supposed to have them. (No mention of any names, but it was not my little one and a half year old son.)

We looked, and we walked, and we walked and we looked.

Nothing.

Suddenly I remembered: I could get into my center, then ask my intuition inwardly for guidance and simply listen.

I also asked **Ganesha** to help me find the keys, since in my experience he is the one who helps people find things.

He is officially the Remover of obstacles—in this case the obstacle of forgetting where the keys could possibly be—and he makes things appear. He moves the obstacles out of the way, so that one can find whatever one has lost.

Using my intuition this way has worked several times in my life, but this one was the most dramatic.

I had literally no idea where those darn keys could be. The beach was really big, there was nobody around, and we didn't stop anywhere. We just walked, walked, and walked.

They really could be anywhere.

I remembered Ganesha, and I said inwardly: "Ganesha, Jai Ganesha, thank you very much. Could you please help us find those keys." I said it inside. I was just going inward.

It was as if I was bowing down to my inner intuition and guidance, with the help of Ganesha, this energy that is already present everywhere, that you have, that we all have, that lets you tune into this energy and find whatever you need.

I was just going within and asking and listening on a very subtle level.

And while I was saying that inwardly on a very subtle level, I walked.

I walked a little bit away from my son and my ex-husband, and just walked, following this inner guidance. I just randomly, seemingly randomly walked in a certain direction while saying this.

At a certain point I suddenly stopped. I looked down. I saw something silvery and shiny. I bent down, I picked it up.

Our keys!

The beach was miles long.

Nobody else was around.

Sand and pebbles everywhere.

We had walked for an hour and a half every which way.

The only way we found those keys was by turning within, to my intuition, inner guidance, and yes, with help of the energy of Ganesha.

We were much relieved as you can imagine.

Here is the picture of that outing, I think this was on the way from the car to the beach, *before we lost the keys.*

It's really that way: **what you put your attention on, grows stronger in our life**. You can develop that skill of your own intuition. Listen to yourself first.

You first. Your own center, your own boss, remember? You already know. You just have to get in touch with it.

And from that center you feel out what you need, for yourself, and more and more for everything in creation. And we're all One anyway, so we can learn to pick up on that.

I hope that helped you. Practice it a lot, okay?

Especially if you don't have any major decisions to make.

Because those decisions will come at you at some point, and then you may feel: "Oh dear, I hope this works. I wish I had practiced this, because now I don't know. Is it just my fear or is it real?"

You want to practice with little tiny things. Just ask yourself little questions you already know the answer to, in order to practice.

Then listen and feel what your body does. You'll notice it.

You're a sensitive human being. You came to this training because you're already a very spiritual and sensitive being.

Simply tune into your body and you'll have the answer.

Have fun!

BONUS #3

FEEL IT & HEAL IT

When You Need a Little Extra Help

For those times, when we find we don't even have the energy to get going, or it feels it's just not enough to do the 7 steps, here's a really effective way to tackle emotional imbalances—let's call them that, shall we, haha—you know the kind: Something makes you upset, sad, afraid, angry, insecure, worried, and so forth. Sometimes seemingly out of the blue.

It may appear to come from someone else, or be triggered by a certain event or situation, but inevitably, if you react a certain way, that reaction comes from **within you**.

First, I have to tell you, the one technique for me that clears out stresses like no other, and makes me feel so much ease and joy, because it connects me with my true center, my Self, is TM, Transcendental Meditation.

It's like the high power washing machine, organic detergent and gentle dryer combined. For fastest evolution and change for the better, try TM.

To learn more about TM, please go here: TM.org

When you're going through a rough period, and need a quick fix, and your shrink is out of town, here is a do-it-yourself relief for you:

For the quick fix **spot cleaner** when you need something specific gone asap, learn how to

- feel what is no longer in your Highest Good.
- dissolve whatever is in the way of you shining your light and aligning with who you really are.
- fill that new void with the power of your own inner Divine Light.

Here is the first tool, and it's a very subtle one.

It involves you sitting down comfortably.

Since you're most likely reading this sitting down, you can do that right now. You can even close your eyes—once you have read this. :)

Become aware of your breath, and breathe gently through your nose—no big taking in of breath. Just normally and gently breathe in through your nose. Good.

Please know that when you breathe in, you breathe in Divine Light. Especially when you breathe in through your nose.

With every inhale you breathe in Divine Light, that most subtle substance the whole universe is made of.

You breathe it in all the time anyway. The whole universe is made of it, there's nothing else beside it.

But when you become aware of it, that's when it becomes interesting. That's when it becomes powerful.

Your attention riding on that breath makes it a healing tool.

So breathe in Divine Light right now and send it into your body consciously, wherever you need it.

Maybe it's your heart, maybe it's your tummy, maybe it's your lower abdomen, maybe it's your neck, your jaw, your tongue, your forehead, or any other part.

Breathe it in very gently, and feel how the air with that Divine Light travels up your nose, maybe slightly above the nose into those resonances you are familiar with, if you're a singer.

Then your breath, with that Divine Light riding on it, goes down into your lungs, and from there into your whole body.

Breathe in Divine Light and breathe it into your whole body, your whole being, with every breath, with every inhale.

Good.

Now this is what you do:

You inwardly as if scan your whole body with your attention. Feel into your body and see where your attention catches. It could be in your leg, your back, your arms, your head.

However, most of our tension, pain, and emotional wounds tend to be in the torso.

Go down inside your body with your attention, as if in an elevator, checking your whole torso: seventh floor, sixth floor, fifth floor, fourth floor, third floor, second floor, first floor, basement, earth.

Be there scanning very gently, and just settle down, settle down, settle down.

As you scan, it's as if **you open the doors of your elevator in every chakra** and even in between, and scan where there's anything that doesn't feel good.

Feel whether it's an ache, a pain, a constriction or tension, any not-good feeling, anything not radiant, wonderful, easy and peaceful. Anything other than at least the neutral spot.

Feel where there's any constriction or some uneasy feeling, and just breathe Divine Light into that.

Breathe it there, and then, on the exhale, simply say inwardly, feel inwardly: "Thy will be done. I surrender. Thank you God, and so it is."

I'm not a big fan of exhaling while intending to "breathe out the bad."

It's more a matter of breathing in Divine, healing Light into the body, and then surrendering. Those two steps.

With that Divine Light—just like we switch on the light and it dissolves the darkness—with that light the darkness leaves automatically.

You can feel it.

If there was a tightness before—maybe in your tummy area—and you breathe Divine Light there, what happens?

You might feel that area expanding a little bit, getting a little bit warmer, a little bit lighter, with every in-breath.

That area of your body just relaxes.

It's as if you can finally let go of those kite strings that have been cutting into your hand, because you're holding onto the kites too hard, and the wind tugs it the other way. You can finally relax it.

What happens? That area relaxes, expands, and feels warm, and suddenly the tightness is gone.

It's as if all the little molecules there drift further and further apart, like many kites disappearing into the sky.

And on the exhale you simply say: "Thank you God and so it is." You just surrender at that point; you just trust.

Breathe in the whole energy, and on the exhale you simply give it up to the Highest, and trust that it's dissolved.

Then *feel* the Light rushing in where the tightness was, and into your whole body. Nature abhors a vacuum. Your own inner Light will fill it with the best possible outcome and manifestation for you.

You can use this mechanism where you breathe in Divine Light consciously, and then you exhale and think "Thank you God and so it is," or "Thy will be done," or "I surrender," in **two scenarios**:

- when you want to **dissolve** something, or
- when you want to create **or manifest** something.

Because guess what?

Divine Light is there anyway. Divine Light is what the whole creation is made of. Divine Light is what all the "not-good stuff" goes back to anyway. After all, what seemed to be not good was simply something that is no longer serving you now. And your very Nature is Divine Light.

You might as well use that creative force not just to spread the light and dispel the darkness in your body, the not good feeling, the pain— but you might as well use it also to create some wonderful new things.

What could those be? What do you want? What is it that Divine Light can create other than the entire friggin' universe?

It can create health, it can create abundance, it can create love, it can create a beautiful, joyful feeling, a warm feeling, or a new car, literally. It did that for me. Remember "The Secret?" Exactly.

Feel Divine Light, the manifesting, powerful energy of infinite Divine Love and Light. You're breathing that in. Every time you breathe. Whether you're aware of it or not. Might as well be aware of it!! And this is what it's like.

We forgot. We were never taught. I was never taught. I had to figure this out. And it came, and now here it is, so make use of it.

Breathe in Divine Light. This abundance of the whole universe, the basis of the whole universe.

Breathe it into this body of yours, and feel the relaxation in the area that is not relaxed. And while it's relaxing say "Thank you God and so it is."

Or manifest what you want. Breathing in this creative, Divine Light.

And here's where the Magic happens:

In the *moment when the inhale switches to the exhale*, that's when the dissolution happens, and that's when the manifestation happens.

In that little gap between inhaling, and then exhaling "Thank you God and so it is," there's a short stop, and that's when and where the magic happens.

It's like the breath comes in, the abundance, the light comes in, and in that tiny, tiny gap between inhale and exhale, that's when the dissolution happens. That's when the manifestation happens.

That's why your attention is so important on anything, any thought, and any feeling.

The more subtle, the more powerful, right?

The Quantum level of existence is pretty darn powerful.

So when you have a subtle feeling you may not be aware of for awhile, and suddenly it's manifesting in your body or in the environment, you have to become aware: "Right, I was operating at a really powerful level, I'd better be very aware of where I'm putting my attention."

Same with something creative you want. On that subtle level where God is manifesting, where Divine is manifesting the whole universe, you can manifest your life.

This is your job. **This is why you are here.** Because you feel that power—you just didn't know how to do it. Now you do.

You have a certain dharma, a certain calling, your own life purpose.

You align yourself with your dharma, and then you learn the tools, how to get crystal clear in your dharma about who you are, why you're here, and what you're here to do.

And then you do it.

You have the tools to get centered, you have the tools to get expanded, you have the tools to enliven yourself, all in 7 seconds (Sing Yourself Well).

You have the tools to listen if something is right or not right, using your intuition (Intuition 101).

You have the tools to make yourself feel loved (How to Love Yourself).

And now you have the tool to dissolve anything on a subtle level that is karmically somehow imprinted in your body (Feel it and Heal it).

If you're done with it, and you don't want that pattern in your life any longer, you simply dissolve it—back to cosmic energy, your own Nature.

Breathe in Divine Light, close your eyes, and on the turning point between inhale and exhale, the magic happens. On the exhale simply say: "Thank you God and so it is. Thy will be done."

It's as if you're bowing down to eternal Divine, which is your own dear nature, and the nature of everyone and everything around you.

It's not a deferent thing, it's not like: "Oh, I'm bowing down to something greater than me."

You can do that too, it feels wonderful. I know I've done it and I love it.

But I love most of all when I'm in my space, in my alignment, in my self-referral, and I do this.

Creating, and saying thank you for it—Creating, and saying thank you for it.

This was the first of the two tools you can use to clear away anything that is in the way of your sun shining brightly—of you being that Divine spark you already have and are.

Here's the second tool. This one is a bit more hands-on manifest, and it really works well.

It's a combination between Jyoti Atman, Light of the Soul—which I learned from Amshiva Malani, private student of the late Dr. Balraj Maharshi, world renowned Ayurveda physician—and what is commonly known as EFT, or tapping.

I've used both of those techniques in my work for seventeen years now, and over these years it's merged into something that's really powerful and really quick. I'm all about condensing my years of experience—25 years of vocal studies and 17 years of healing—plus several hundred clients, healing- and voice students, to make everything accessible and easy to use for you!

If you need a quick fix, and you just don't have the time, the space, or the privacy to close your eyes and go inside, feel, dissolve and create, then this is something you can do that's very quick and works. (You may still want to do it in private just because people may look at you funny.)

This is how it goes: you may know there are meridians and meridian points throughout your body. For this technique, you can just pick a few important ones, and you tap on them.

I always tap on them with my middle finger and ring finger.

You simply tap on these points to enliven them. Then tell your body, in just one or two words—or even just on the feeling level, once you've done it often enough:

"**Dear Body**, thank you so much for all you do for me. Right now I need your help dissolving this old program of yours that you've got going and that you got me running around for years and maybe lifetimes! It's time for a new program. And this is what I would like from you."

This is basically what you're telling your body when you do this.

You're nice about it—but you're very, very clear, okay?

If something doesn't feel good in your body, and you really need your body to release it, then this is what you do:

You tap between the eyebrows on the third eye, about five to seven times, then you tap on the side of the eyes, you tap under the eyes, and you tap on your sternum.

Last but not least, you tap on the two points below each of your collar bones. Pay special attention to these.

At the very end you hold your left wrist with your right hand and your right wrist with your left hand for a few seconds each, while you say out loud: "Peace, Love, and Light." Or conversely: "Thank you God, and so it is!" Again, that surrendering, light-filled feeling.

The reason I do both wrists just like in the self-love exercise, is that it's good to balance out both sides.

While you tap each point you say something.

STEP A:

This first bit is what you say when you have a little bit more time:

"I'm releasing all karmic impressions and illusions that are no longer in my Highest good. I'm letting them go now. It's safe to let those go now."

And then you grab your wrist, and say: "Peace, love, and light. Peace, love, and light." Or: "Thy will be done." Or: "Thank you God and so it is!"

Alright, let's do that one more time just for practice and then you can think of something that you actually want to dissolve.

"I am letting go of all karmic impressions and illusions that are no longer in my Highest good, and dissolve them into cosmic energy now. I'm letting those go now. It's safe to let those go." On the wrist you say "Peace, love, and light. Peace, love, and light." Or: "Thy will be done." Or: "Thank you God and so it is!"

Feel **everything you're saying**. *Feel* the peace, the love and the Divine Light coursing through your body, which it always is, of course.

Basically you're just coming back home. The right side, the masculine side, grabbing the female side reassuringly, and the female side grabbing the masculine side reassuring it that everything is well.

That was step A of that technique. You dissolve what you don't want. Your body will say "Yes, Ma'am."

Step B:

Now you fill that vacuum you created with things you do want, right?

So you tap those points again, saying: "I'm now invoking Divine Light to manifest the patterns of perfection for my Highest good, and for the Highest good of all others concerned."

Then you hold your wrist again, and say: "Peace, love, and light." You can also say: "Thank you God, and so it is." Whatever feels really good in your body.

The reason holding your wrist is so powerful is that the heart meridian goes through there, which is why we also touch there for Ayurvedic pulse diagnosis and feeling the pulse. There's a heart connection here in the wrist.

Also when you hold your own wrist it actually feels really yummy, it feels really sweet. So you want to end with that: "Peace, love, and light. Thank you God, and so it is."

Now, think of something that you don't want to feel anymore. A pain, sensation, or emotional tension in your body that doesn't feel good to you.

Maybe it's a tummy ache, or a constriction around your heart, or you're shy, or you just always feel off when you go to a certain place.

For instance, I don't particularly care for socializing in public.

I'm fine on a stage in front of thousands of people. I'm happy and comfortable there.

And I'm very happy one on one or in a *very* small group of friends or family.

But actually going out, being in restaurants or at a party, it's not my thing, never has been, may never be. Just hanging out for the sake of hanging out is not my thing.

There are times when I have to go out in public and socialize, and then I do this technique.

Now do it for you.

Whatever your thing is right now, something you're simply done with. Something that may or may not have served you for a while but now, you just don't want it anymore.

Feel it in your body, feel where it is. Is it in your heart, in your tummy, in your throat? Feel it. First feel it, remember?

Feel it, and then heal it. Okay, good.

Feel it, and then tap. "I'm letting go now of all karmic impressions and illusions that are no longer in my Highest good, in that area, in that particular incident, in that part of my body, and dissolve them into cosmic energy now.

I'm letting them go, and it's safe to let them go."

The reason we say it's safe to let them go, is that sometimes the body holds on to a pattern it's familiar with for dear life. That fear is usually stored in the kidneys.

Remember I asked you to pay special attention to the two points underneath your collar bones?

Well, those two points are the meridian points for the kidneys. The kidneys contract, if there is fear. They hold fear, and you have to tap and reassure them and say: "It's safe to let that go."

Because the body likes its old way even though it may be crooked.

Your body/mind may say: "Yeah, I know, but this is how I'm used to walking and I'm comfortable. I'm okay, I don't want to be shaken up."

Believe me, you want to shake it up. You want to make it floppy, flowing and moving. You want to make it free and high and low and everything in between.

You want to have all the tools in the world, so you don't hold on to anything. Especially not to things and experiences that cause you pain.

But, on some level the body will say:

"Well, I'll let go of all these things, but that one thing no, no, no, I really still need that. I want to hold on to that. Just bear with me there."

Sometimes it'll be really sneaky—everything will feel clear, you've dissolved everything, you've manifested Divine Light—but you can feel that there's still something hiding, like a little gremlin in the corner, and he's just hoping you don't see him—that you don't discover him.

Feel into your body, by using the elevator exercise. Go down the elevator, feel where there's something not in alignment, that doesn't feel good, peaceful, free and flowing.

Then either dissolve it quietly inwardly, or if you're in a rush simply say: "That thing. **That little gremlin: I see you.** I let go now and remove all karmic impressions and illusions that are no longer in my Highest good, and dissolve them into cosmic energy. And it's safe to let them go. Peace, love, and light. Thank you God, and so it is."

Once it's dissolved, always end with manifesting the Good, breathing in Divine Light, and manifesting: "I'm now invoking Divine Light to manifest the patterns of perfection for myself, and for all others concerned, in the Highest Good for all."

This feels really good, and you know what else you can say? "It's safe to be me." Because it is! Who else would you rather be?!

When you invoke Divine Light to manifest the good you want, at the end tell the kidneys: "It's safe to be me. Peace, love, and light. Thank you God, and so it is."

Now you have a tool box you can open any time you need to. A whole smorgasbord to assist you in becoming healthier, happier and more vital.

Enjoy becoming more of who you already are.

Again: Conclusion and Send Off!

So this is what the 7 Second **Sing Yourself Well** System, the 7 Second Reset, does for you. Yes, of course it increases your lung capacity, and strengthens your immune system, releases endorphins and makes you happy. But clearly, as you now realize, the magic lies in more than that. This 7 second system

- Centers you in yourself.
- Helps you relax your breath in the most natural way.
- Aligns you with Heaven and Earth.
- Opens your body to health and flow.
- Enlivens frictionless communication between the different parts, the energy centers or Chakras, of your body.
- Establishes you in your own power.
- Energizes your body and spirit in a fun, efficient and profound way.

There is no way your brain can maintain an emotional downward spiral, when you apply these seven, very **physical tools**.

Within seven seconds your body will be reset by you to come back to at least a neutral position. With your own breath and voice.

Usually my clients, students, and kids I teach in schools tell me that at the end of those seven steps they are bouncing up and down, they're laughing, they're *joyful*, they have their energy back up—and they can't wait to continue with life before it got all dark and weird!

So learn those tools, practice them, and use them.

You then have a means—any time something wants to pull you below the surface—to get back up really fast.

And that is the key, that is the beginning of clear thinking, clear feeling, being in your center, and being in your power.

Then you can make better choices, choices for more energy, for better health, for better habits, for being around the right people, for taking the right action steps in your business, for all these many expressions of yourself, for all your creativity.

But you have to come to that neutral point, and have the tools to come at least to that—as fast as possible.

I'd be hard pressed to tell you if there's anything I've found that is faster than the 7 Seconds **Sing Yourself Well** System.

I clearly have not come across it because otherwise I'd be peddling that! :)

But this is something I've developed in my seventeen years of research, of teaching, of self-exploration, of performing, of having clients, and of teaching students.

Those seven steps are unbelievably powerful, and I cannot wait to hear from you what your experience is, how many times you use them, and how it's helping you.

Plus, now, if you stayed on for the bonuses, you have additional healing tools to get you into a better place, fast. After all energy is what everything is made of. Clear yourself energetically, and then set your own frequencies vibrating within your body.

As you realize now, singing has benefits way beyond increasing your lung capacity, strengthening your immune system and making you happy.

SING YOURSELF WELL™ IN 7 SECONDS

It profoundly changes the way your body-mind-spirit connection functions, which in turn has profound benefits for how you feel in any given moment. As we know, we only ever really have this moment. If we make the best of it, the future takes care of itself.

So start today. Start in this moment. If you don't like this moment, use the 7 steps and in 7 seconds take charge of the moment from that more neutral place.

Who knows, maybe you're now on your way to a whole new you. Maybe your appetite is whetted, and you can't wait to sing more, play more, and attune your body to the grand cosmic symphony, all because you woke it up to its own, inner energy, and frequency.

That's what had happened to me.

There is of course much more, and we barely scratched the surface in this book. If you'd like to know more, or find out about any upcoming training, feel free to register and get onto the VIP list at SingYourselfWell.com.

And if now you're really discovering your own voice and want more training, I'll let you know when my **Ultimate Singer's Guide** as well as **The 7 Second Reset**™ are coming out. Again, just get onto the VIP list at SingYourselfWell.com.

I'll see you soon, and in the meantime: Sing Yourself Well!

Love and Light always,

~ Ulrike

For the accompanying **Sing Yourself Well**™ video training, all 7 steps (the 7 Second Reset™), plus 7 bonuses (3 hours total), go to SingYourselfWell.com.

You can watch, listen and follow along. Plus if you want to refer back or fast forward, you may do so at your leisure.

See you there and Sing Yourself Well! :)

~ Ulrike Selleck, Healing Voice Expert

Acknowledgments

First and foremost:

Thank **you,** dear reader, for investing in this powerful and vitally important guide to learning how to use your voice and change your life. This book was written with your joy, health, happiness, and vitality in mind. Please share it liberally with your friends and family.

This being my first book, I will indulge in acknowledging the heck out of who was and is important in my life.

First and foremost I humbly bow to the Almighty Divine Source, my true home, my real Self, Nature, One-with All, and loving guide within.

My deepest, unending gratitude goes to my spiritual teacher and guru Maharishi Mahesh Yogi, his teacher Guru Dev (who in my awareness seemed particularly keen on my getting this knowledge out there), and the Holy Tradition. In my first hour of darkness, with yearning in my heart, Maharishi's Transcendental Meditation technique brought me back to life, and I owe it everything. I will feel forever blessed to have had the great honor, blessing, and privilege to spend two and a half years around Maharishi, and to have become a teacher of this priceless technique.

Next, I want to thank my beloved family of musicians, singers, teachers, artists, writers, merchants, and scientists:

My energetic, creative, and loving mother who was a classical singer, musician, artist, choir director, music teacher and conductor for over 50 years. While I was recovering from surgery after a cancer scare (the transformation that inspired this book), having taught voice for years herself, she sent me written voice lessons all the way from Germany to the United States, via fax.

To her last day, which came suddenly and too soon, she was my trusted friend, and an inspiration for all my endeavors.

My wonderful, heart-based father, a physicist and editor, who did everything he could for our family and never stopped sending me little, lovingly wrapped Christmas packages to the States until he unexpectedly passed away a few years ago. I miss you dearly, Pa.

My loving, genius, and thankfully also goofy brother—a physicist and editor, after my father—who has the gift of making me laugh even when I feel down.

I honor and thank every one of the 50 members of my entire extended family, including my dearest aunts Ina, and 97 year old Traudel, and her daughter Ursel, who owns and manages an awesome bookstore in Germany.

My beloved son, Girindra, who is a lawyer currently living in NYC with his wife, who's a school teacher, and was once—between the ages of 10 and 12—a professional opera singer starring in several operas. Thank you, too, for lending me your brilliance in editing this book.

My former husband of 23 years, Thomas, who's often helped me out with input of his decades-long direct marketing experience.

My love Mark, who fearlessly plunged headfirst into the process of us building a little cabin on the prairie, and who, with his caring nature, inspired me to believe in myself from deep within myself, through all trials and tribulations.

Furthermore I want to thank my dear friend Amsheva Mallani, who taught me the energetic healing system of Jyoti Atman, passed on to her privately by renowned Ayurvedic physician Dr. Balraj Maharshi.

I give my wholehearted gratitude to the many saints I've had the great honor of meeting in my life: Beloved Maharishi, of course, and also Babaji, Sant Takar Sing, Karunamayi, Mother Meera, who generously gives daily online darshans, and Ammachi, who, with her beautifully devotional, heartfelt songs, inspired me to pursue my vocal career.

My wonderful, talented, and kind former voice teacher, the formidable baritone Professor Stephen Swanson.

The world-famous mezzo soprano Cecilia Bartoli, with whom I feel such a connection, and who inspired and encouraged me to sing, even though I was already in my mid-adulthood.

My best girlfriends Christiane, Lisa, and Teresa, who with their love, wisdom, and acceptance have helped me through both, my darkest and happiest moments selflessly and compassionately over and over again. I love you dearly. And of course my many dear friends, who have put up with me promising them a book for years now. Thank you. :)

My beloved Mother Earth, and the many animal and plant friends, my 9 kitties, who seem to know when I need their gentle, yet committed purr the most; and the deer, birds, bunnies, eagles, hawks, herons, dragon flies, butterflies, owls, and frogs. I love you all.

Finally, I want to thank Dr. Deepak Chopra, Ayurvedic physician par excellence, motivational speaker, and author of dozens of best-selling books. Dr. Chopra came to me in my second hour of darkness and lovingly showed me the way out of it. Without him, there would be no book—and possibly, no me.

.

Inspiring resources you might enjoy

Meditation: Transcendental Meditation: tm.org

SingYourselfWell Youtube:https://www.youtube.com/@singyourselfwell

Nonviolent Communication: nonviolentcommunication.com

The Success Principles, Jack Canfield

Elayna Fernandez: thepositivemom.com

Dr. Deepak Chopra: deepakchopra.com

Marie Forleo: marieforleo.com

Brendon Burchard: brendon.com

Great Singers on Great Singing, Jerome Hines

Eckhart Tolle: eckharttolle.com

Nia Dance: nianow.com

Yes to Success, Debra Poneman: yestosuccess.com

Happy for No Reason, Marci Shimoff: happyfornoreason.com

Powerful and Feminine, Rachael Jayne Groover: rachaeljayne.com

The Soulmate Secret, Arielle Ford: arielleford.com

The Passion Test, Janet Bray Attwood: thepassiontest.com

Conversations with God, Neale Donald Walsch: nealedonaldwalsch.com

ULRIKE SELLECK

Marianne Williamson: marianne.com

Loving What Is, Byron Katie: thework.com

The Secret, Rhonda Byrne: thesecret.tv

www.ingramcontent.com/pod-product-compliance
Lightning Source LLC
Chambersburg PA
CBHW070756100426
42742CB00012B/2155